Dedication

This book is dedicated to my precious little boys. You remind me daily that life is messy and beautiful all at the same time. That even though I cannot control most things, I can control how I respond. So when I look around at all the mess, I am reminded that I do not have to let the mess become who I am. You deserve better, I deserve better and the other people in this world who need me, need all of me, not the constant hot mess me.

Thank you, Jesus, for the hard but sweetly humbling opportunity to be a mom.

NO MORE HOT MESS

Remember Whose You Are

Cheneil Torbert

2018

Contents

Introduction

NO MORE HOT MESS

Remember Whose You Are

Greater is He who is living in me!
He has conquered our enemies!
We can stand here in victory!

James 1

Consider it pure joy, my brothers and sisters,[a] whenever you face trials of many kinds, ³ because you know that the testing of your faith produces perseverance (James 1:2-3).

⁴ Let perseverance finish its work so that you may be mature and complete, not lacking anything.

⁵ If any of you lacks wisdom, you should ask God, who gives generously to all without finding fault, and it will be given to you. ⁶ But when you ask, you must believe and not doubt, because the one who doubts is like a wave of the sea, blown and tossed by the wind. ⁷ That person should not expect to receive anything from the Lord. ⁸ Such a person is double-minded and unstable in all they do.

⁹ Believers in humble circumstances ought to take pride in their high position. ¹⁰ But the rich should take pride in their humiliation—since they will pass away like a wild flower. ¹¹ For the sun rises with scorching heat and withers the plant; its blossom falls and its beauty is destroyed. In the same way, the rich will fade away even while they go about their business.

[12] Blessed is the one who perseveres under trial because, having stood the test, that person will receive the crown of life that the Lord has promised to those who love him.

[13] When tempted, no one should say, "God is tempting me." For God cannot be tempted by evil, nor does he tempt anyone; [14] but each person is tempted when they are dragged away by their own evil desire and enticed. [15] Then, after desire has conceived, it gives birth to sin; and sin, when it is full-grown, gives birth to death. [16] Don't be deceived, my dear brothers and sisters. [17] Every good and perfect gift is from above, coming down from the Father of the heavenly lights, who does not change like shifting shadows. [18] He chose to give us birth through the word of truth, that we might be a kind of first fruits of all he created.

I hope you are ready to dive into some goodness sister by being obedient, but most importantly I hope and pray that you will have an open mind and open heart and willingness to take action in the areas that you know the Lord has already called you to.

I've been on a journey to freedom and I have learned a lot about myself and my life. I have also learned a lot about our Heavenly Daddy and his unconditional love for us. So my prayer in this book is that you are able to hear truth from my life and my experiences and see Jesus, His truth, and love for you as we uncover some ropes that maybe you don't want to even take off. Maybe you are "comfortable" or maybe you are "scared" of what this might look like.

Listen, we are in this together. Nothing is more defeating than to KNOW the Lord is calling you towards something and you are continually not doing it. And nothing is more liberating and freeing than to experience His love, and know that you are taking the right steps towards His plan and purpose for you and your life.

A Note from Cheneil

Hey beautiful sister! I am so glad you are here. I am so thankful and honored to get the privilege to share my heart and a few things Jesus asked me to share with you. I want you to know that I have been thinking about you and praying over you for months. I want you to know that this book was a lot harder than I expected to get to you today. The enemy worked really hard to not make this happen, but I believe that was because I needed to go through yet again another struggle to come out on the other side seeing even more of God's goodness. I also think it's important that you know that what often seems easy on the outside or in the highlight reel of social media is probably not what is assumed. I have come to expect the struggles just as much as I expect God to see me through them. So I hope you are ready to dig in, peel back some dried up layers, cut some ropes, and destroy some old name badges you have been wearing. I hope you take the time to not only finish this book, but actually think through the application sections. You know I gotta help a sister out with some real-life action steps. So grab a notebook and a pen. I prefer something bright and colorful so that you are excited to use it every day, but that's just me. The big picture here is that you will see Jesus in all of your mess, see how much you are loved, and begin to see yourself, your life, and the hope you have in him a little differently. And through this, you BELIEVE. Because what we know is that your life is truly a reflection of your strongest belief. Either positive or negative, good or bad, what you believe is how you live. My prayer is that you are reminded of who you are and whose you are and you BELIEVE!
Let's do this sister!

High fives and hugs!
Cheneil

Preface

No more sitting back, sister!
I cannot allow you to do this any longer.
I know your heart!
I know that you have wanted to say YES for way too long
and I want to help you!
From one sister to another, in love, it's time.

If I know you well enough, you probably have at least one
thing on your heart that you have been wanting to do, to
start, or complete. You have probably started many things
but can't think of many, if any, you have finished.

One of the things I struggled with for years was reading. I
told myself I hated it because it was hard, that
comprehension and attention issues would prevent me from
enjoying it. And well, I would rather be doing something
active. I had never experienced life on paper. So, I just never
finished or had any interest in finishing a personal
development or spiritual development book.

I would be willing to bet that you have 'reading' among your
list of 'must finish' or on your 'to-do' list, but you can't seem
to find the time to start or just can't seem to finish. Or maybe
you have finished a few books, but you haven't completed
that craft project, or that house project, decluttering efforts,
or maybe you started your dreaded healthy lifestyle journey,
but with your kids and your job or your lack of support...
well, you can't seem to get started. Or, you have been self-
sabotaging because you have not managed to stay committed
to any efforts you begin. Or maybe your marriage desperately
needs help, but like other things, you are too exhausted to
put out any more effort. TV, another glass of wine, sleep,
another sports activity, another bag of chips, another project

to attempt, another group, another friend, these things seem to keep you feeling "ok" about life. But deep down, you know something needs to change, don't you?

Even now you are wrestling with something.
You might not be an "extremist" about it, but the little messes of life that you have told yourself you are really good at living will either pull you apart or keep you in a place that will only cause you to look back on your last year and think, 'What the heck has happened? What the heck have I done? What is wrong with me? Who am I?'

You probably feel the internal battle. You hear one voice coming from one shoulder and one coming from another. Something pulling one arm onto the couch, into contentment, begging you to get all cozy and comfortable even though some things aren't quite right, and there's another something pulling your other arm trying to get you off the couch, and with a big old squeeze of the face and kiss on the forehead saying, "Hello!!!! Do you not get it?! I love you and we've got things to do, places to see, people to meet, and I don't want you to miss out! Let's go!"

This battle. We are all experiencing it EVERYDAY!
Paul is the guy in the Bible that we can count on to firmly nudge us in the way of truth. Even though we might not like what he has to say, he is so helpful, isn't he? This internal battle that I mentioned above, one arm being pulled one way (flesh/law) and the other (spirit), the other way, Paul had the same battle, y'all.

Romans 7:15 says, "I do not understand what I do. For what I want to do I do not do, but what I hate I do."

Deep down, I want you to know that we are all a mess. We all have this inner battle going on. It might be with different things, from different perspectives, but we all struggle.

One thing I have learned through my time working with amazing people as a nurse practitioner and lifestyle coach is that there's a lot of searching and looking, listening, reading, hoping, even praying and begging to make this "thing" go away, to get better, to make sense of it, to fix it, longing to experience something different or something to change.

We want a change of circumstances, change of attitudes, change from people, change from within, right? We all have this battle and we all want something to fix it, don't we?

So how do we fix it?
What do we do?

I want you to know that I certainly do not have all the answers, and the ones I want to offer might not be ones that you want to hear. But I wholeheartedly believe that you are here for a reason. You are being pulled in many directions with all the roles that you play, and you are tired. I do know that I have a solution, some things that I know will help, but I am going to need something from you so that I can point you to these things.

I need attention. I need willingness. I need effort. I need BELIEF.

Attention. Cheneil, do you realize the kind of life I live and how much of my attention is already taken?

Willingness. I am willing Cheneil, usually am, but it depends on what exactly is required. Remember, I am busy.

Effort. Oh, hold up, wait a minute, you want me to put some BOOM in it? Effort? Because you know, I don't have time for much.

Belief. Oh, you are really asking a lot, Cheneil. I mean. That's pretty far-fetched.

So many thoughts are going through your head right now. But I want to preface this book with what I need. Why? Because you matter to Jesus and to me and he wants to share some things with you so YES. This will require some work. And I promise it will be worth it.

So, let's do this THANG sister.

Chapter 1

When Hotmess Hits the Fan

So often, as soon as change requires any DOING on our part, we turn the other way. Mentally, we start thinking of reasons why we should NOT. We start rationalizing thoughts that were not right to begin with. We dig our heels in and point fingers. We use our past or our situations to become excuses. Most of you, yes, statistics say that 90% of you reading this book, will be super empowered after reading, like a summer-camp-high, and then do nothing with the information given. NOTHING. Why? Because you might need to grow, you might need to think, and you will need to take action to make improvements. But so few are willing to take action to improve.

Let's do a little checkup, shall we?
Let's talk about your LIFE right now.
How do you feel?
Are you at peace?
Are you fulfilled?
Are growing and learning?
Are you using your God-given gifts?
Do you feel free?
Do you feel enough?

Most of the things that we desperately search for are right in front of us, but we are so bogged down and overwhelmed that we cannot see them or hear them and therefore, we panic, which either looks like a full-blown anxiety attack, self-sabotage, taking it out on those you love, or closing off and avoiding. But something happens y'all. We can't pretend that life goes hunky-dory, because it doesn't. Or maybe on the outside it appears that way, but on the inside, not so much.

You know the quote, if overthinking burned calories I would be skinny? I mean hello! So true, right? Not that being skinny is at all what we need to be, but I think it is safe to say that most of us find ourselves in a state of constant of feeling overwhelmed and over internalizing things. Perhaps because we don't feel that we are living up to a crazy expectation that we created, we are worried about what other's think, or we simply add more things to our plate to make us feel better and more in control. Or sometimes we just let go of it all and let ourselves go in the process in hopes that all the pieces just fall into place or work themselves out. But sister, let's be real for a second, it doesn't really work this way does it?

Instead of seeking and just BELIEVING in ourselves, in the process, and in God, we question everything.

And in the mess of it all, there's always something that we need to do, some sort of action that we are being asked to do. Even seeking requires action, sister.

But here's the question:
Are you willing to take the necessary action?

And you know what, this was me, questioning everything, doubting my purpose, His plan, and my capability, even just a few months before completing this book!

Chapter 1

I thought I was exempt from so much doubt, fear, and feeling overwhelmed. I never imagined that the enemy would be so intentional with his attacks on me, my mind, and my heart, and I certainly didn't realize that at times I had even let this fear make me lazy by not meeting deadlines and not sticking to what I had committed to doing. I am one that when I make up my mind, I do it! I resist the weight of challenges and keep fighting and going until, well, even my body fails like it did a few years ago. I take action, y'all.

But then something happened. It's called LIFE. Just like the one you live. LIFE. And my mess hit the fan. And then splattered throughout every part of my life. Kind of like what happens when your toddler has a poopy diaper, feels it on his leg, and proceeds to spread it onto EVERYTHING within arm's distance.

Yes, that's kind of what life felt like. A big, ridiculous, pungent, mess. I felt more out of control than I had in a while, and out of control usually sends a message to my head and heart that I am failing. Usually this starts with, "I am failing as a coach or business owner." Then it starts spiraling out of control to, "I am failing as a mom or wife." It doesn't have to be in that exact order, but if I am not careful, one area of insecurity can quickly lead to another area of disappointment and failure.

So month after month I was telling myself that I was not capable. I was obviously failing at the roles that I was entrusted, because they weren't doing as well as I thought they should, so since those things were failing, what on God's green earth made me believe that I could possibly be a writer, too? And if I decided to go for it, then I would fail at that, too. And as things spiraled, every ounce of my life was impacted by what I wholeheartedly believe was my lack of belief, which resulted in my disobedience. Both of these terms will be used interchangeably in this book because if you don't believe, then you are not living in truth. Right? When you don't believe truth, you ignore it, you turn the other way, and you do the opposite. And God's truth is our way to freedom. Understanding His love for us is our way to freedom, the freedom that he died for us to have.

In my opinion, if you don't believe the truth, it will seem impossible to live in love, and most often you will live in a state of fear, whether you know it or not.1 John 4:18 says there is no room in LOVE for fear. Well-formed love banishes fear. And this, my sister, is hard. Well-formed love means we BELIEVE this TRUTH so that we can live in love, love for God, love for ourselves and love for others.

So, this was me.
I said 'Yes' to my hotmess month after month because I was living messy and most things were truly out of my control. But living in the mess of life lead me to tell myself that I was indeed a mess by rationalizing and glorifying this to be my truth. I even bought the coffee mug #hotmess mom, so of course, I started believing this.

I did what most do when we are not sure what to believe, or we are wavering in our belief system. Like that thing that pulled you onto the couch, you end up believing something, either a lie or the truth. And if you are like me, the lie is much easier to believe. So, I did grab hold to what I thought seemed more like me at that moment. I grabbed onto the lie. The lie that my house, my thoughts, my marriage, my business, my life is a mess, so I am a mess.

Chapter 1

I am a hotmess.

The problem is, the storm keeps raging. When you are living in a state that is not true to who you are, the storm doesn't stop. Just like it doesn't stop when things are going well. I could not shake this feeling. I knew something had to change.

Maybe you have spiraled out of control lately, too, and feel like this is you! You either want to stay here because it's easier, or you feel desperate to move, but you just don't know how. Or my dear friend who just doesn't know what you want, I will help because I love you. We all must do something! No matter what position you are in, there is action to be taken.

If that's prayer and the Lord hasn't quite answered you, you still must pray. If that's rest and removing some responsibilities, then you must remove them. If that's paying more attention to areas that you have neglected, like your marriage, then you better be more intentional. If that's stopping eating out every day of the week so that you can start feeling better and more in control, then you better stop eating out. If you are confused and feel distant from life or your relationship with Jesus, then it's time to make time for Him. There is action to be taken, no matter what.

And after months of me believing the lie "I can't," I took action!

I was still fearful, overwhelmed, dealing with guilt, shame, and insecurities, all the MESS y'all. I was a big, bold, HOTMESS, but I made a decision. It was a scary decision and I BELIEVED.

I knew, in the deepest part of my soul, that I was asked to do this by the Lord. I knew I believed in God and YES, I believed in myself too. You are holding this book and reading these God-inspired words because God has spoken to me, day after day. When I allow myself to listen, he talks to me through people and things. When I look, I see him everywhere.

So I know God's truth, and I made a decision to STOP allowing the enemy to win. To stop allowing the hotmess to win. Not because I don't still feel like a complete mess or have doubts and fear, but because I know that my God is capable of much more than I am. The Lord has things to say through me, and he was waiting for my willing hand and heart to write what he wanted to say to YOU through me.

He had been waiting for months for me to just let Him do what he wanted to do in and through me. He NEVER needed perfect or ready; he just needed me to be willing to open my mind and heart and move my hands and feet. But most of all, he needed me to BELIEVE. Believe in myself and believe in Him. And here's the deal, you cannot believe in something with every part of your being and not take some sort of action. Your inaction means you don't believe.

As I was willing to start listening and hearing from Him, Jesus sweetly reminded me about the imperfect actions that are already part of my life, like my morning Jesus time, my morning workout, the efforts I put in my marriage, sacrificial efforts as a mom, and the encouragement and motivation I provide daily. He was right. I already do hard things because I BELIEVE they matter.

Chapter 1

I absolutely do not do these things because they are easy or that I always want to do them. Things like making healthy meals for my family, waking up at 4:30 in the morning to allow quiet time with Jesus, getting a good sweat therapy session in before the kids get up, cleaning up house when it seems like it is constant and never-ending, saying NO to the desserts or cocktails at girls night out when everyone else is taking part, missing out on many activities because I am planning for my next month's online accountability group, having late nights and bold conversations, and not watching TV because sleep is more important or reading a book will benefit my heart and mind more. These things are not always fun, but I believe these things matter.

One really hard thing was asking my husband to go to counseling again because I felt emotionally neglected and stagnant in our relationship. I do a lot of hard things because I BELIEVE these things matter. I also believe that how you do anything is truly how you end up doing everything. And NOPE, it's not always sexy or fun and definitely not always easy. But it matters.

You matter. Your life matters. The simple, mundane, unfun things, just like the big things, matter. And guess what, they all matter tremendously to God. Colossians 3:17 says to let every detail in your lives – words, actions, whatever – be done in the name of the Master, Jesus, thanking God, the Father, every step of the way. I hope that you are thinking about your own life and all the things that you do, giving yourself some ridiculous credit, or maybe you are thinking of the things that you don't do or want to do. This is not a book about making you feel guilty and to just add more things to your list to feel better. Oh no, sister. This is about taking a step back and taking the chance to see what is actually going on. Maybe you need to move, but maybe you need to be still and listen. I don't know what that is for you, but I do know that you want peace in your head and in your heart. Most call this happiness. You just want to be happy.

But unfortunately, it's not as easy as that, is it? Often what we think makes us happy also becomes the root of our unhappiness, our hotmess as I like to think of it. This pursuit of happiness in perfection or self-satisfaction, when pursued from a place of fixing ourselves or fixing others, will never allow us to be completely satisfied, happy, at peace, or free, sister. And that's usually how we live, that's usually the path we are all on. We strive for the number on the scale, the resolved body image issues, the perfect family, the perfect intimate connection with non-bargaining attention and good, fulfilling sex with our husbands, the dream job, the amount of income earned, being present, more and more time with kids, the recognition, the validation, the appreciation. We are hoping that when I achieve "THAT" or when "THAT" happens, then I will have the peace, my soul, longs for. Then I will be happy. I will then be free.

But what happens when you feel like you have everything under control? For once in a long time you are having a great week and then you realize: wait, there are some really big things off of the to-do list. The house you just picked up is a wreck again. You didn't have time to look at yourself before you left the house in the morning and you are mortified by the glimpse you get of yourself in the mirror this evening. So the good week quickly spirals and all the things, especially what you see in the mirror, leads you to remember that you haven't had sex with your husband in a few weeks, maybe months, and suddenly YOU become the reason. You are the reason that EVERYTHING is a mess. The reason that you can't keep a handle on the house, the to-do list, the business goals you are not meeting, and the list could probably go on and on and on. Maybe your routines are off. Your life gets messy and your mind becomes a mess, too. You are overwhelmed, anxious, and have started saying those old self-sabotaging things you used to say, and well, you are believing them. You realize that even your "me" time and your "Jesus" time is not happening.

I was a complete mess. I knew it. I thought that I could do better. I thought that maybe I had better control, I thought that I was better. But clearly, I was a hotmess. I can't be loved. I can't do anything. I won't ever do anything. Who am I? What have I become?

We are all longing for that one thing that will give us peace and happiness, but when we don't get that one thing, or it becomes hard to get what we want, or when we actually do arrive there, we don't feel as satisfied as we thought, then suddenly the glimpse of hope we once had is ripped away and we start all over again. You start all over again.

The hotmess! You arrive here, time and time again, on the couch being pulled down one minute and being pulled up the next. Over and over and over. Don't we? It's exhausting. Spirit Crushing. Soul Squishing. The glorified hotmess life is kind of like that beautiful, colorful, hot pink cupcake that you know will heal all of your wounds and make you forget about life for a second. Then you take a bite, and it's stale, it's NOT buttercream, and it tastes like rubber mixed with mothballs. We have all had that disappointment, right? This is so frustrating because you probably passed on something else really amazing for a crapcake.

Chapter 1

The hotmess life is just that; just like eating a crappy cupcake. It doesn't deliver, doesn't satisfy, doesn't give you the feeling you were hoping for, and then after you eat it comes the worst part. You feel yucky, guilty. You wish you would not have eaten it. And the strangest thing happens, you feel empty again. Well, because you have been here before. And clearly, I have too, many times because I compare life with cupcakes. And I have binged on many before. But the truth is, I actually believe that you can have your cake, the good, good life God wants for us, eat, and experience freedom, fully, too.

It's definitely not like the skinny tea, the keto diet, the no-eat diet, the faux eyelashes, the cute jeans that were on sale, the quick gratifying FIX. Experiencing LIFE is NOT a quick fix. I have never believed in these or encouraged these because of THIS exact reason. It's like the cupcake that we just talked about. Somehow these things make us feel good and maybe even look good for a short amount of time, and then hotmess happens, and you are back at square one.

So when I told you that we will have work to do, action to take, I meant it. I never said this was going to be easy for you, just like writing this was not easy for me. But sister, I love you dearly, and I want to make sure you understand how much your heavenly daddy loves you, too. So if you stick with me, I PROMISE that it will be worth it. And when we meet, and I get to hug your neck, we will enjoy a delicious cupcake together in honor of you finishing this book and taking action in your life.

If I can do this, if Jesus can do this through me, then GIRL! He has some amazing things for you, too. You just have to BELIEVE.

Chapter 1

I hope you are ready to dive into some goodness sister, but most importantly I hope and pray that you will have an open mind and open heart and willingness to do what YOU need to do to have the peace and FREEDOM you crave in the areas that you know the Lord has already drawn you to, so that you can live in His freedom. This is not the freedom the world talks about that involves stuff, I am talking about the kingdom peace and heavenly freedom that will last forever.

Since I have been on this journey to freedom, sister, I have learned a lot about myself and my life. I'm still learning every day, too. I have also learned a lot about our heavenly daddy and his unconditional love for me, and I know it's so important for you to get it, too. So my prayer in this book is that you are able to hear truth from my life, my experience, and from the words of our daddy and others I have had the privilege of walking with. I pray that you would see Jesus, His truth, and BELIEVE his love for you as we peel back some layers of your hotmess life.

Maybe you are "comfortable" or maybe you are "scared" of what this might look like. Listen, we are in this together. Nothing is more defeating than to KNOW the Lord is calling you towards something and yet you continually circle back to where you started or look up and despite all the mess happening around you, you realize that you had never moved.

The core of who we are longs for connection, intimacy, belonging, hope, and to be loved. So, if you are drawn to more, long for more, or different, or feel unsettled, know that this is how you were created and it's beautiful. Your journey to love can be found in knowing and understanding God's love for you. And there you will find truth and freedom. He is wanting to go places and take you along with him, guiding you one step closer to His plan for you: freedom.

And let me tell you, there is nothing more liberating and freeing than to fully experience His love and know that you are taking the right steps towards His plan and purpose for you and your life. As your sister and friend, I cannot withhold truth and love from you! When we encounter the Lord, there is always an opportunity to let our encounter be someone else's by boldly sharing. It can be what someone else needed. I have been asked to boldly share. We have been given this responsibility to share truth.

I know when I first started my own deeper walk with my heavenly daddy, I didn't like some of our conversations. For example, I didn't like the ones in which he was saying, "I get it. I know you don't want to, but I am going to keep running after you and throwing things at you that you can't avoid until you say 'yes' because this is your best and I want you to experience it," or the conversations we have had about waiting and trusting. Yep, I am a control freak and asking me to wait is like adding fuel to my hustle, making me want to figure things out even quicker on my own.

Maybe you are thinking of conversations you've been having, or not having, with Jesus recently or over the years, and you haven't been too happy with Him either. Or maybe you have felt angry, confused, and believe he has forgotten about you. Or maybe you are on the other side of confusion, anger, disappointment, or pain, and you are thankful for where he has brought you, and you are excited to start taking steps forward.

Or maybe you are right in the middle and thinking, Cheneil, I just don't know how I feel. I am unsettled, I am discontent, I know I am not living up to my full potential, and some days it bothers me and others it doesn't. I have been in all of these seats and the one thing that I can say is that although we change, waver, and allow situations and things to persuade our thoughts and actions, HE has never changed.

For JESUS never changes – yesterday, today, tomorrow, he's always totally himself. Hebrews 13:8. Despite me and my hotmess, you and your hotmess, who God says I am and who he says you are, has never changed. If it's been a while since you took a look in the mirror or read about what Jesus has said about you, let's take a look at a few truths that he calls you!

Please take a second to affirm this truth.
Place your name in the blanks (write out each affirmation).

Example:
Cheneil, You are unconditionally Loved (with every ounce of my being, PERIOD!)

_____, you are worthy of love, forgiveness, freedom, peace, and abundance. (John 8:31-32, 36)

_____, you are valued, worth more than any earthly thing. (Isaiah 43:1)

_____, I gave you unique qualities, and I want to help you use them. (Romans 12: 6-9)

_____, Intentionally trust Me to provide for you, every moment of every day. (Luke 12: 22-28)

_____, I created you just how I need you to be to live out My purpose. (Philippians 1:6)

Take another look at this truth for YOU; who you are! Look how amazing you are to our Mighty God! Sister, he loves you so much and he has some extraordinary things he wants you to be a part of with Him now, while we are waiting to spend eternity with Him in GLORY.

I mean, if He makes sure that the birds of the sky are taken care of and paints the side of the highway with beautiful wildflowers, things that we don't even pay attention to most of the time, think of how much He cares for you! (Luke 12:22-28) STOP right now and think about this for a second.

You are beautifully, intentionally, and wonderfully made. He pieced you together so carefully with specific things for you to do, and then said, "I will not leave you or forsake you, instead, I promise I will come live in you and do it ALL through you." (Hebrews 13:5-6; Deuteronomy 31:6) This was a promise. He does not take you lightly.

No More Hot Mess Mantra:

I am sought out and well cared for-

Luke 12: 22-28

This is such a beautiful thing. Oh, it's such a beautiful thing. It took me many years to actually BELIEVE this. I believed a lot of things, even developed a pretty deep belief in myself until life got real messy and I showed up in a place of emptiness like I had never felt before. I was confused and

lost; I was a mess. And maybe you know Jesus, you have heard his truth, thought things were ok between you and Him, but then life gets messy.

Abuse
Affairs
Neglect
Debt
Kids
Lost Job
Infertility
Failing Health
Death
Anxiety
A busy schedule
Guilt
Shame

The mess of life happens, doesn't it?

And despite knowing Him, His truth, His love, before we even realize it, we often decide to choose self; our comfortable self, our frustrated self, our pain, our selfish desires, our own plans, our selfish wants. We even chose other people or what they think over Jesus, and they become most important. (Galatians 1:10)

We find ourselves in a place where we look around and our stuff, our situations, our pasts, our doubts, and our fears overwhelm us and ultimately, our MESS somehow matters most. This messy life that we so quickly relate to, live in, and even subconsciously encourage, support and ultimately settle for, this HOTMESS life becomes LIFE. Or I like to think it becomes the only way we feel we can live life.

Chapter 1

Trust me! I believed it, too. Believe it or not, NO ONE is exempt. What I learned about my experience is that the hotmess life is nothing more than another scheme of Satan. It is another way to deceive us into being someone we are not. I believe deception is one of the biggest missions of the enemy. He is deceiving us into believing we don't matter, that we are insignificant, that we are a mess and better there, among many other lies.

So when the busyness of life, the mundane, pain, guilt, shame, the overwhelming stuff makes you believe that you are indeed a hotmess, this is not a surprise. We need to recognize that this is exactly what the enemy wants you and me to believe. Because if you believe that you are a hotmess, then you now have a "reason" to lean in to. We can now use the things that are causing the MESS in our minds, our homes, our body, to be the reason why we stay stuck, why we don't take action, why we settle, and ultimately, why we are constantly longing for something, but constantly feel lost and incomplete.

Instead of letting Jesus be our source, our reason that we can or should do certain things, we let our mess be the driving force in our life. Even though truth tells us that because of Him we are more capable than we can ever imagine, we let the mess convince us otherwise. Instead of believing and living out our truth, we let our Mess becomes the reason why we can't, shouldn't, don't have time, are not capable, are not smart enough, and are not disciplined enough. Instead of living out our truth KNOWING that God has our back and best interest, even in the hard things, we live in our mess and we let our mess become who we are.

But sister, I don't know if you are ready for this, but WE DON'T HAVE TO LIVE IN THE MESS, and I will no longer let you be there! I am confidently convinced that WE are more powerful than the mess! The lies that the enemy feeds to us do NOT have to dictate our lives or cover up who we really are, y'all!

So instead of wearing the #hotmess badge (or the t-shirt) with honor, it's time to crush that badge, throw it away, and put on your CROWN.

No More Mess:

- If you haven't figured out, Satan is alive and well and doesn't plan on resting anytime soon. He wants to destroy YOU! So yes, he is going to keep you busy, exhausted, overwhelmed, frustrated, and empty. He is going to keep reminding you of your pain and hurts, and you better believe he is going to turn every molehill into a mountain that you feel you cannot climb. Because he wants to keep you in your mess. In your mess, you are both too distracted to hear from God, and you are exactly where you need to be to hear from God.

- Think about your life, Right now.
    - In spite of your chaos, your overwhelmed, your frustration, your pain, the stuff of life, God is speaking to you.
    - Do you hear Him?

- In my own personal experience, I get confused when navigating next steps or when previously trying to work through issues with a counselor, as well as during times as a lifestyle coach when I was helping women take action. We all get confused. We know Truth, but we can't tell if the Lord is telling us something or the enemy is trying to distract us with something else. What I can tell you is that our God is NOT a God of confusion. (1 Corinthians 14:33) He never has been and never will be. So, when you feel like God is trying to tell you something, he IS. The confusion is usually us trying to avoid God's voice or avoid the work that comes with the request.

And if you start thinking of all the reasons why you can't or why you shouldn't, you are listening to the enemy. Now I am not referring to circumstances of obvious distractions; I am talking about when the Lord is asking you to make a change in your life and it is GOOD, something that will positively impact yourself, your family, your future. Hello!!! It is of the Lord.

Quit using the excuses of your lack of faith and trust. We have to stop! This is EXACTLY where the enemy wants us. He wants us to believe that he can steal all that God has given to us. He wants us to doubt our gifts and calling, God's love, grace, and forgiveness. Even though we know the truth, he wants to keep us from believing it and living it out. 2 Corinthians 11:3 says that "But I am afraid that just as Eve was deceived by the serpent's cunning, your mind may somehow be led astray from your sincere and pure devotion to Christ." When we believe the lies of the enemy, that all we are is a mess, there is a good chance we will not live out God's design for us because the enemy has deceived us into believing that we can't.

Chapter 1

When the Lord asked me to write my first book, a devotional, He used a mentor to tell me that I should do it. I thought it was crazy at first. Let me tell you, I could have used every excuse from working crazy hours as a nurse practitioner, experiencing basically no sleep, running a business, and raising two preschool boys who needed my attention. I don't have any formal training on writing, I have attention issues and could never sit down to write, I had so many excuses waiting for me to grab onto. And yes, I even said I would "pray" about it, because that's what we all do when we really don't want to do something or believe it's possible. We make ourselves feel better by at least saying "I will pray about it" and just maybe, if and when I did make time to pray, God might show me something I didn't see. Yes, I use that tactic a lot too when I just don't want to do something. I had content ready that needed to be placed in a book so that others could read it and see the truth that I had been reading. God brought someone to me to help me see His plan. This is probably something he has already done for you as well.

He has probably already placed things on your heart and people in your life, but you are not seeing them for what they are. You are using your busy schedule, not being ready, not having time, YOUR MESS, as excuses. Yes, I too, thought it was crazy. Yes, I knew it was going to be hard and out of my comfort zone; basically everything in my life has been hard and crazy. And NOW I know it is of the Lord because crazy and hard will require His help. Easy and mundane, well we can all pretty much handle that. This book, like other things, when I really thought about this from a kingdom perspective, is something He wanted me to do and if I didn't do it, there might be people who miss out on Truth and Hope.

I HAD TO DO IT!

I had to shut down the lies. I had to affirm my strength in Christ and believe that He wanted to do this through me and I had to DO IT!

So, if you KNOW, because I know that you know, whatever the Lord has been asking you to do, it's time to do it!

- Stop and Pray. Talk to your heavenly daddy. Like really talk to him. Tell him the lies you are believing.
- Swap the lies for the belief that He will do what he said he would do.
- LEAN into it and go for it! Fearlessly go for it, knowing He is guiding you.

Chapter 2

I Can't

Consider it pure joy, my brothers and sisters, whenever you face trials of many kinds (James 1:2)

I will live not on the basis of what I can't do, but what God said HE WILL DO.

I can't. I can't. And let's be real, I can't even believe I am writing these words. I am NOT an "I can't" kind of person and I do not even allow these words to be spoken in my home. But, YES, "I can't" is what I was saying for weeks and months! WHAT!?

Maybe you find yourself saying this often, too. If so, l am so glad you are here because we have some work to do, but if you know me at all, you know that typically NO one or nothing gets in the way of me doing something I feel passionate about. To say that I allowed fear, doubt, being overwhelmed, and insecurities that the devil himself created in my head to control my thoughts and actions, is humbling to even admit, sister. I admit I was embarrassed. I was supposed to be the ultimate motivator I acclaimed to be.

But I, too, allowed "I CAN'T" to have complete control over my thoughts and my actions. I think most of this is because I began to doubt, and this doubt covered up my belief. I doubted my role, my abilities, my future. I even started comparing and found myself in a place that could have completely changed the trajectory of my life. I could have stayed there, in the fear, doubt, being overwhelmed, and insecurities, and looked back months and years later wishing I would have completed this book. I could have done this.

As fear had set in, the enemy was literally screaming in my ear like a banging gong that I had misunderstood and made up all of this in my head. That I wasn't capable of being used, of doing this. That God did not really ask me to write this, it was just something I had made up to make myself feel better. After all, I had left my very expensive medical career to pursue Jesus' plan for my life and anyone who would do such a thing is probably a little messed up in the head. Anything that would require that much work is probably not going to work out. I was listening to the enemy and began to make up my own lies.

And then I stopped. I let fear take over.

Maybe you have things in your heart, too, that you KNOW you need to do, but have spent days, weeks, months, years listening to doubting thoughts and lies from the enemy and just can't seem to take action. Or maybe you get a gust of hope or revelation on Sunday or a post on social and you head full-force into making changes and then something happens. LIFE happens and again, you have a setback, a disappointment. You start believing that if this is THIS hard, then maybe I am not supposed to do it. If "I" can't make this happen, then maybe I am just supposed to be. Be how I am, accept where I am and eat the ice cream, swipe the card, refuse to talk to my spouse, continue to beg God for change, but accept that maybe I can't have it.
And then let it go.
Or NOT!

It's not that easy, is it? Can you really quit thinking about these things?

If you are being asked to do something, if the spirit is nudging you to write a book, to improve your marriage, to start a Bible study, to teach a fitness class, to start a business, to move to a different town, or to adopt a child, then you already know He is asking you to move with Him. Are you actually listening or just ignoring him? God does not stop pursuing us or offering His help because we don't want to do it or we don't see it for what it is. You play an active role in what's next in your story, the place God is calling you, and this doesn't stop just because life gets hard or because you refuse to take the necessary action.

Sister, God has written a story and invited you in it. He has planned a magnificent ending for you, and many others, but he wants and needs you to be actively involved in His story. He believes you are worthy and perfect enough that he invited you in with a specific role in mind and for a kingdom purpose.

So when you feel something stirring in you to make a change, HELLO!!! It is because God needs you to do this so that He can show you something and bring you to your next chapter. He NEVER said he wanted you to live in the same chapter of your life forever, nor does he want you to live in such a mess that you can't even see what He is trying to do in and through you. We could all easily live an entire HOTMESS life and wake up one day realizing we have missed, literally missed, life. He NEVER intended for you to grow old wishing things could have been, would have been. He does not want us to spend our entire life in neutral.

Chapter 2

My heart breaks to know that there are so many people who will go to the grave with regrets. Some subconsciously and others willingly living their entire life under the bondage of fear, doubt, being overwhelmed, and having insecurities, using hotness as a reason why we can't experience the life of freedom that God has for us.

How do I know this will happen? Because this is exactly what the enemy lives for. The truth is, the devil himself cannot control our destiny. When you said YES to Jesus, you already have your name written in the book of life and you will spend eternity with Jesus. YES!!! Praise God.

But listen to me, since the devil cannot control your destiny, he will do everything he can to deceive you and keep you from being actively involved in the work of the Lord here on earth. He can keep you from being used and living in complete freedom and peace here on earth simply by throwing things at you that make you doubt everything about yourself and your entire life. He will intentionally use conversations, actions of others, the inaction of others, situations, the list goes on. He is probably trying to deceive you right now as you are reading this book, especially the next time you go to pick it up and read, he will likely start telling you that you are "ok." You don't really need to finish this book.

Trust me, this stuff happens all the time. He loves to make you misunderstand, misinterpret and allow your thoughts, the lies, to become your reality. If he can't control your final destination, you better believe that he will do EVERYTHING in his power to keep you from living out your purpose, your passions, and a life of love and peace here on this earth.

A few years ago, while listening to a sermon, something profound stood out to me. I know I had heard it before, but for some reason I did not get it before. I finally got it. Check this out y'all. The Lord is writing a beautiful, powerful legacy, a life-giving and redemption story, and allowing me to be in it. That day, in that sermon, I heard it and it changed me. I believed. From that time God has continued to do a mighty work in my mind and heart and I knew that I needed to share my journey. The good, the bad, and the ugly. Stories and topics that are hard but needed.

When I would sit down to write this book, I wrestled with thoughts about how this would look, what to say, comparing my style, and wondering how I would catch your heart and attention. How was I going to help you see truth and love? After taking your precious time to read this book, would you close this book feeling closer to Jesus, viewing Him as someone who loves you dearly and wants a blessed and abundant life of freedom for you? Would you receive this and believe this so much that you would be empowered to take action? YES, I said take action! This is my heart!

That you see Truth and you then take action. Don't be a back row Jesus girl, letting others be the voice and you sometimes be the echo. No, my heart is that you hear and see truth and YOU JOIN ME AND BECOME A BRIGHT, BOLD, AND LOVING VOICE.

And THIS! It HIT me like a ton of bricks. It became more real when I was saying "I can't" to writing this book. God is asking me to share something HE wants to share. It's not about me. He wants to use my story, my struggles, the divine victories he has allowed, the words in this book, to help you! He wants to use me because he knew YOU would be willing to read it, and through this book you will learn more about Him and His truth and you CAN have victory, and peace, and FREEDOM in Him if you received it and are willing to take action.

And guess what? If I chose not to take action against my fears, my insecurities, my doubts, the unknowns, then you would not be reading this book. But the more time I spent in prayer, being woken up at night, looking at the mommas in my online communities, my mom's groups, I continued to be overwhelmed with YOU, your heart, your life, your family, your dreams, and your legacy. What if the holy spirit himself speaks to you, through me, and causes a holy fire to burn and causes YOU to change, you to see Jesus in a different way? Then your life will change and other lives are impacted.

You better believe that I could not stay seated anymore.

Let me tell you, sister, it grieved me so much to think that because I was choosing not to write and share my passions, my heart, the things I have learned, my struggles of life, love, and hope, that someone might miss out on Jesus or truly understanding His love and His plan. When we are called to do something, I believe that it is because God wants to use us to share Him. It's not about our capabilities or fanning a flame on our talents. Doing what he has called us to do is about sharing Him with others, which brings people closer to Him and also brings us His peace and joy, which is what we all long for, right? I longed for this peace. I knew what I needed to do, but I wasn't doing it. And to think someone else might be able to see and hear and know God better if I would be brave enough to trust and write a new perspective of faith and trust and honoring what I had been asked to do, not because I was capable, but because it was something God wanted to do through me. I cried an ugly cry, y'all, thinking how much this must be grieving my heavenly daddy that I would believe that I was not capable to be used in this way. I believe that THIS is the kind of life he wants for all of us; a life where we are ready and available to hear what God is asking us to do each day and we are willing to trust him, have the courage to step into whatever this may be, and regardless of how impossible it might seem or how incapable we might feel, we trust and believe and walk with Him.

NO, you don't have to write books, be in front of people teaching, sharing, or be in "church ministry." You don't need to compare and think you need to do anything that others are doing. You only need to care and worry about what YOU need to be doing. The reality is, your story matters. And there are people all around you, every day, that would benefit from hearing from you.

Your family, first and foremost needs you! The Lord graciously gives us our family because he wants to use us to minister to each other. He believed that we were so important that he gave us our spouses and our children, even our parents, so that He could work in us and be Jesus to them. And you better believe this can be a very daunting and overwhelming thing, but this is where His Love and His spirit come in. Our belief is in His power, not in what we can do. But y'all, when we refuse to take action, we are willingly saying "NO." We are willingly walking in fear, in our insecurities, in our doubts, shame, and we are believing that we are not capable. But more than that, we are calling God a liar.

In Christ, we are not punished for what we don't do here on earth, for it is by Grace we are saved and loved and invited into heaven, but I do believe that we miss out on things and YES, others miss out, when we choose not to walk in love, in trust, in belief, in faith, in obedience. Jesus does not need us, but instead, he chose us.

Why do you think the Bible says we are HIS hands and feet? Because sister, he wants to use us.

No More Hot Mess Mantra:

I am the hands and feet of Jesus-

1 Corinthians 12:27

This will look different for everyone, but it's true. And that means he wants to use you! As a matter of fact, I believe that he is waiting. He has probably been trying to show you something, hoping you will hold onto it and start talking with Him about it. Or maybe your life has been such a MESS that you haven't been able to see or hear what he is trying to tell you. We have all been there, distracted and fully living up to the hotmess, pretending that you want to stay there, knowing and feeling your heart is being pulled to something greater, something more. More peace, more freedom.

I know you are longing for this because so was I.

Let me first say that you are LOVED, oh, so loved sister. Can you affirm this truth with me? I am unconditionally LOVED! This is your truth: that NOTHING is tied to His love for you, not your work, not your shortcomings, not your past, not what you aren't doing right now… NOTHING. You are unconditionally loved.

No More Hot Mess Mantra:

I AM UNCONDITIONALLY LOVED-

John 3:16

The Lord is here and wants you to get that. I am asking that, with an open heart and mind, you would be willing to allow the Lord to speak to you. Be willing to see where you are and where God wants to take you. Consider taking off the #hotmess badge. Can you do that for me? Pinkie swear? Cross your Heart?

Ok! Let's go girl. Before we start, can I be real with you for a second?

The purpose of this book is not that you just softly travel through reading the words and then allow yourself just another chance. A little more grace. Yes, I said it. I love you, but I do not want you to keep giving yourself more reasons not to change, knowing it's not right. NOPE! No more.
This book is about seeing truth, believing truth, and living out truth.

I will not be the friend in your life that gives you permission to:

- go after that dream in your heart LATER when you feel better equipped,
- give yourself a little MORE GRACE since you've committed to a healthier lifestyle, but you keep

starting over and have decided to believe you just can't take control,

- quit your marriage since it's constantly underwater and it seems "he needs to change" so you continue in bitter resentment for another 14 years of marriage,
- forget the dream in your heart for women coming together, to support each other, grow and learn together. Yeah, it is a crazy dream, so you should quit thinking about it,
- forget about your child that you have been longing for, but you're too scared to adopt and you keep pushing the feelings back because of fear,
- quit writing because it got hard and it must not be what God wants for you,
- quit school because there were too many other things on your plate, or
- believe that you are insignificant that you don't matter, that you will never be good enough because that's what you were told for years, allowing your abuse to be who you are.

NOPE! I will not give you permission to continue to wait, quit, or forget. I am not saying that there are some very significant reasons why someone is where they are in life. Please know that I am in no way trying to be insensitive to horrible things that have happened to anyone. I understand that life can be very painful; there is abuse, loss, illness, and mistreatment, all very hard and significantly impactful.

But I believe that using these hard things, the pain, and the misunderstandings as the reason not to LIVE life is not how God designed us to live. I believe that these things are likely the direct path we need to travel, pointing us to the Lord so that we can allow Him to work in even the hardest and darkest things and places in our lives. (James 1: 2-5) And I believe that this just might be the road to healing and helping he has been trying to take you on all along.

I love you and I care about you and not only do you deserve the joy, abundance, and peace that is waiting for you, but your Jesus died a painful, undeserving death for you to live in freedom, not to live in chains.

Now I know what you are thinking: WAIT! God tells us to trust Him, and Cheneil, you just don't get it, I am tired, I am over it, a lot has happened to me. And you have no idea what I have been through or have already done. And hey, what if I frankly just don't want to do anything right now, I believe the Lord said, "be content" and "rest in me."

I hear you and I know that God's timing is truly perfect. And maybe the timing of this book isn't for you right now and I am ok with that. Just like I tell my lifestyle coaching clients, I will never beg another person to improve their life, but what I will do is be HERE, with arms open wide when you are ready to take the first steps.

But for those of you here and willing to take the first steps, consider this book your HUGE EMBRACE, from me and from your heavenly daddy, gripping you tightly, whispering, "YOU'VE GOT THIS because I've got you!"

No More Hot Mess Mantra:

I have the grace to embrace every season of my life-

2 Corinthians 12:9-10

Chapter 2

It's time to quit running.

It is time to stop living on the basis of what you can't do and start living based on what God said HE WILL DO.
It's time to grab your armor, pull up your big girl panties, and stand FIRM in His love and truth and YEP, you got it. It's time to take action. I did, now we are here together, so let's do it!

I want to help you! You are SO MUCH more than your mess! So it's time to say #NOMOREHOTMESS

No More Hotmess

It is time to stop living on the basis of what you can't do but what God said HE WILL DO.

Like I said, I believe that the Lord is here and his truth is on these pages. With an open heart and mind, I know that he will speak to you. If you are willing, he wants to take you to some amazing places.

No More Hot Mess Mantra:

I am strong-

Proverbs 31:17

When I first began to hang up my coveted #hotmess badge, I remember battling my inner voices. I know it sounds crazy, but many mornings as I was starting to give Jesus time, I would read His truth and it would very much contradict what I had been telling myself for years. I would be so overwhelmed with the negative things I was telling myself and the truth that I was living in that after reading and writing

Scripture I would usually go workout because I always considered this as a continuation of my therapy session with my heavenly daddy. My workouts started to become a little different. I used them as the battleground to fight out the lies. I would visualize all the lies and frustrations and punch them into thousands of pieces. I would see myself pushing past and crushing the lies as I pushed myself harder, challenging myself, all while telling myself TRUTH. And y'all, I still do this today. This has been life-changing and I believe that fitness is just another act of obedience, a way to honor ourselves before the Lord. Being obedient and grateful for our health, mind, body, and soul is something we can do to be ready for anything the Lord has for us (Proverbs 31:17.) And If you haven't had a fight with your old self, the lies, your inner negative Nancy, or Satan himself, oh you should! It makes for a really amazing, sweaty, freeing workout. You should try it soon.

But if you aren't into a therapeutic sweat sesh YET, (I say yet because my prayer is that you will be open to this soon) then you can start fighting back with the words that you are saying to yourself. I do this during my workouts too, because so often we are actually speaking lies over our lives all day every day. I had no idea this was so impactful until I listened to my first podcast recommended by a friend and she basically said that your words have power. What you are subconsciously saying to yourself, 'I can't,' 'I won't ever,' all the things we just talked about above, they become your truth. Whether you want to believe them or not, if you are telling yourself these things, then they are how you live. You make decisions based on what you are telling yourself: fear, doubt, shame, and that hotmess that you have now identified yourself with. I realize that it might have started out with your comprehension struggles, past struggles, or your stinkin' pile of laundry that seems to never get folded. But these things, the mess in your life, does not mean *you* are a mess. You have mess in your life, but your identity is not in this mess.

And y'all, this took me a lot of repetition. I had a lot of mental blocks, and still there are days that I find myself thinking lies and suddenly I am behaving in a way that is not in line with WHO I AM.

One of the most empowering exercises that I have been taught is affirmations. I would hear these things, see them on Pinterest, and feel connected with them, but often shut them down until I was lost. I literally felt so alone and so lost. I knew Jesus, but I didn't get Him. I was introduced to an author and speaker through a podcast and per her recommendation, I started affirming His truth. I didn't realize how much of the things I was telling myself were lies and how much this was actually impacting my life. I started reading and writing out TRUTH like the Scripture was directed at ME. I was affirming God's truth and writing it out and saying it out loud as my new truth, all while asking God to keep my eyes open and mind ready to receive His truth. I never doubted my salvation, but I definitely felt that there was a distinct difference in how I received God's word and lived my life when I started to seek and see God's word every day. It started to become TRUE, my reality.

This time with Jesus becomes part of my morning every day. Normally I would "sweat for Jesus" and this was my priority. I always felt great and empowered to be a good "Christian" the rest of the day, but there was something missing. After a few years of starting my day with Simply Jesus, affirming His truth, writing out His truth, my truth, I felt the tug of the Lord to keep coming. To follow him. Not sure what that really meant, I started listening more and he guided me to my first book, Miracles in the Mess, a 90 Day Affirmation Devotional. He wanted me to share my heart and put the things God had been showing me on paper.

After I got my first copy in the mail, I knew it was God's little gift to me that I could then gift back to Him through sharing with you! So if you journey with me through Miracles in the Mess, then you are affirming your truth every day.

If you are not on that journey with me, you will get to do that here in this book, too.

I will admit, at first I thought these "feel good chants" were a bit corny and well, "not something I needed" or had time for. But just like everything else in life, we don't see the importance or the impact until we do it. Sometimes doing the thing that we know matters, will positively impact your life, and what we don't want to do is the very thing that we need to do to change our life. So I am asking you to have an open mind.

What I do know is that what I was saying and living by was wrong, it was not working, and it left me empty and striving and unhappy. When I started reading, writing, and affirming God's truth, it changed me. This practice of affirming His truth has become the cornerstone of where I am today and the changes that God has been wanting to do. They have become my belief system instead of all the lies that I was telling myself for so long. I had to learn to reprogram my brain with His truth and believe it. I know this will be true for you if you take the time to receive them the way God intended for you to receive them.

I am worthy – Ephesians 2:10

I am the hands and feet of Jesus – 1 Corinthians 12:27

I AM UNCONDITIONALLY LOVED – John 3:16

I have the grace to embrace my weaknesses – 2 Corinthians 12:9-10

I am strong- Proverbs 31:17

Affirm His truth below. Write the affirmations from above along with the Scripture that goes along with them. Go ahead and after you write them, journal your thoughts about them. How do you feel when writing them or how do they make you feel? Is there anything that the Lord is telling you as you read this chapter? Is there anything you have felt you need to do?

_____

_____

_____

_____

_____

_____

_____

_____

_____

Chapter 3

Fill in the Gaps

I am a voice of encouragement.

1 Thessalonians 5:11,14

I said "yes" to Jesus when I was seven years old and baptized with my sweet momma. I remember my pastor Brother Bruce, coming to my house and drawing the bridge of salvation on a piece of paper and asking if I understood that accepting Jesus was the way to heaven. He explained that he chose me long ago. So I said "yes" to Him and then publicly professed my faith in Jesus through baptism. I remember standing in the waiting area behind the pool in an old sanctuary. I was brought to church for as long as I can remember. I ran around the church behind my granny as she was dancing and shaking a tambourine.

Of all the Christians that I have experienced in life so far, my dear granny, Sister Barbara Ann, has made one of the most significant impacts on my life. I experienced her boldly and passionately speak in tongues over someone and my brother did an amazing impersonation of her, so we often laughed it off. I loved my granny dearly and never doubted her sincere connection with Jesus. Although I never understood her, I just knew that this was her way of intimacy with Jesus. In my eyes, the tambourines and dancing were just part of the Jesus party.

I spent a lot of time with granny growing up. I usually stayed with her while my parents worked on weekends. I went on a lot of road trip vacations with her and my great-grandmother, so I got very close to her. She was a get-up-and-go granny. She was always taking me places, always very particular about her needs and wants, and pretty stubborn, if I might say. Usually she got what she wanted, so I am always reminded of her when I see my mom dig her heels in. I catch myself doing this often; it is a sweet reminder of the gift of stubbornness that my granny left in us.

One of the really awesome things about spending all my time with my granny was that I got to see her minister to a lot of people. She was not on TV and didn't write books, but sister Barbara was a minister. She lead Bible studies in her home and other's homes, boldly sharing her love for Jesus and their need for him with people at a gas station or in the store.

She was always so kind, so loving, bright-eyed and welcoming. One of the most impactful things about my granny is the way she loved and prayed for my family and me. There was a lot of turmoil and darkness that hovered over our home growing up. The enemy was always waiting to use anything he could to cause distress and I believe he was trying to do everything he could to make us turn away from Jesus. When my parents met, they were not Christians. They met at the club y'all. So now you know why I love to dance. It's truly in my blood. But as two young people who enjoyed the party scene, there was lots of craziness that was going on early in my parent's marriage.

Chapter 3

And then LIFE happened. Loss happened.

Years later, I learned that my mom was pregnant before me with my sister, but at 20 weeks delivered a precious child that had already gone to be with Jesus. Her name was Brooke. And I am so excited that I will get to meet her one day when our family will be united and whole.

But despite the sadness, a really amazing thing about God and about my granny is that they had a talk. My parents decided that I would be given my sisters name, Brooke, but the Lord put it on Granny's heart to combine my parent's names, Cheri and Neil, and I would go by Cheneil, which is my middle name.

So, many details of my granny intertwined into so many pieces of life. Although I have to say my name multiple times, it's always spelled wrong and said wrong. I truly believe that God used my granny's influence from the day I was born. This is my reminder that I was beautifully unique, and when I forget, all I really have to do is remember where I got my name and whose daughter I am.

I remember a year before my dear granny went to be with Jesus, she had become frail and was living at my parents' house. She tried to be strong and wanted to care for herself in her stubborn spirit and didn't like to be away from home. But she needed help. We were visiting that holiday weekend and I could just sense her weary soul. She was tired. I think she knew she didn't have much longer. After having lunch that day, we were listening to my brother play his guitar and sing. It was a sweet time. After a few songs, granny called me over, grabbed my hand, motioned for my brother, and everyone gathered. I was sitting hugged up next to her in her chair holding her hand. She began to pray and let the spirit take over. Although I did not understand what she was saying, I am confident that the Lord did. It was like she was commissioning us to continue her legacy of faith.

I cannot explain this, but I felt something in my soul, like an electrical current that shot through me during this prayer experience. I had no idea what it was. I just cried a gut-wrenching cry and knew she would not be with us much longer. I felt a deep sorrow.

A few years after she passed, my mom gave me one of her Bibles. It's the one I use every day while doing my morning routine. You might have seen it on my Facebook or Instagram stories. It has so many personal touches in it, including little notes she wrote to herself, cards that were sent to her, and all kinds of sweet little gifts that I get to enjoy. Even the smell reminds me of so many years with her in her house.

I look back on that supernatural spiritual experience with my granny. It was one of the last really personal and intimate experiences that I had with her. I am not sure what anyone else felt that day, but for me, I believe that God was using her to commission me into a new world of ministry that evening, the one I am doing today. It wasn't until a few years later that I would make this connection.

I was already in the mission field as a nurse practitioner, a wife, a neighbor, and a mom, just like you are doing whatever you are doing right now. We all are. But I had no idea at that time that the Lord was going to call me away from medicine to walk with Him down a different path. But every time I open her Bible every morning, I am reminded about that day that she wanted us to know how much she loved us and how much Jesus loves us. I believe she was asking us to cling to Jesus and to not turn our back on His grace, His love, and His goodness. She knew the struggles that most of us had and walked with us through so much; she was saying hold steadfast to Jesus and He will take care of you.

I am not sure if you have ever had such an experience, but I believe that I started looking at life and looking for Jesus differently. My life did not change that day because of this experience, but I knew something was off with the way I was living life and I know that something changed.

I thought I was living "right" and I had been working really hard, like I was supposed to be doing to be a "good Christian," but I knew something was off. I was a new, exhausted mom just back from maternity leave and I wasn't even sure how to begin. I felt so lost. I honestly felt lost. I felt like I had been running my own long-distance race; I had crossed the finish line, but I didn't even know how I got there or why the heck I even wanted to go down this path anyway. All along I just knew I had worked hard. I knew God was in it somewhere, but I had never stopped to look up (except when I needed to pass a test). I had run a long, hard race based on a decision to live a dream that I felt would provide me with freedom that the world had promised. Freedom of time and money. Something I felt my parents didn't have, so you better believe I wanted to find that.

As I think about so many years of doing the "right thing," the "good" Christian things, my type A personality helped me look real good. I looked pretty good.

But I can say that for so long, I did not KNOW Jesus. I had blamed my lack of reading the Bible or doing many things to get to know him better on my attention and comprehension problem. This girl might not be able to recite a ton of Scripture from memorization, but if you put it to a good beat and I can dance to it, I've got it. But seriously, I didn't really understand God's love for me, what his unconditional love really meant. All I knew and believed was that church, respect, tithing, submission, and working hard were all things you did because you were supposed to. And if you wanted good things to happen to you, well, you better do more of those things, with extra effort. And you know what, God gave me a go-all-in personality, so working hard, doing more, being better, I felt like it I had it down. I did it.

But something was missing. Something major.

I thought that my foundation was strong and that my belief system was strong enough to stand up to life, the mess that would inevitably start happening. But something wasn't holding up. I wasn't as strong as I thought I was. God seemed inconsistent. My small issues, like body image, sense of control, my intimacy struggles in my marriage, my sense of worth as a mom since I was working so much, the issues that once seemed smaller or less impactful, seemed to have a greater impact. The mess started to happen, and I didn't know what to do.

Chapter 3

Maybe you have found yourself here before: growing up in church, knowing the fundamentals, knowing truth, feeling less and less in control, feeling more anxious and overwhelmed, and finding yourself feeling lost.

Why and how does this happen?

For me, I lived in light of who I thought I had to be to earn the good life. To earn favor, to earn love, acceptance. God made me a choleric. If you haven't ever taken a personality test, I enjoyed the most recent one I took, Wired That Way. It basically confirmed my fierce lioness behaviors. I was reminded in this personality test that yes, my personality has positive benefits, but there are also some weaknesses that are inevitable. Regardless, God made me this way. I mean I know this, but oh how sweet it is to be reminded that your heavenly daddy knew exactly what he was doing right.

Being a bit of a lion was my nature before I accepted Jesus. I am a performer so that I feel important. I am an action-taker to gain results that, again, make me feel worthy, important. I find gratification and often identify in what I do. So naturally, I spent years proving I was good enough, proving I was worthy enough.

I am not saying this is what God wanted me to do with my personality, but I am saying I failed to understand exactly what he needed me to do. I was so busy trying to either figure out what I was doing wrong, trying to fix myself, or fix others who weren't seeing things like I was or living like I thought they should. God gave me this personality because he had some amazing things he wanted to do through me. He wants to use me, but since we have freedom of choice, I get to choose how to live.

It wasn't until a few years later that I would make the connection.

In case you are saying, "Cheneil, clearly I don't need to keep reading because I am certainly not a lioness and don't plan on becoming one," we will take a quick look at some other personalities because I think it's fun and might give you insight as we continue on this journey.

You might be saying, "But Cheneil, I am a sanguine (happy-go-lucky monkey) and just want to have fun, I don't need to do anything with huge purpose, and if it requires too much, I just need it to be fun."

Or I am melancholy (an observant owl). I definitely don't get excited about much, and would rather not, actually. Attention of any kind, performing, yeah, that would make me run to my room and not come out for weeks.

Ok, I am a phlegmatic (a supportive teddy bear). I just need peace on earth. I need things to be simple and not require much effort. I don't think God really needs much help.

The point of this is that most of us don't stop and look around. We go through the motions of life. We think we know, but we have no idea. We coast. We live comfortably in our own will and then LIFE happens. I was that person. Even though I had said "yes" to Jesus many years ago, I lived life my own way.

Yes, I was doing good. I was helping people, just like many of you. But I was on autopilot. It was work, home, a Bible study here, church there. For me, I couldn't even be consistent at those due to my schedule in healthcare. I felt like I was just here and one day I felt completely lost.

I was ashamed; I was embarrassed. I thought, "How can this be? I have a great job, one people dream about, a beautiful home, I have a husband who loves me, a new baby, I have it all. Why do I feel so empty?" I couldn't shake it. I began to focus on what I had done wrong to cause this. I began to focus on spiraling out of control emotionally and spiritually.

An inner battle began, something I couldn't explain to anyone else, but I couldn't avoid the discontentment I was feeling. I became miserable and it was affecting my entire life. My thoughts became so dark. I felt drawn to hopelessness even though I knew that was not true. But I kept being drawn there.

I remember just a few short years ago, around 3 am, walking the halls trying to stay awake in the ER. The lights were dim, it was one of the shifts where I could actually stop moving for a second. I was walking around to get coffee and it was like I was in a movie! Everything was in slow motion, everything so dark. I even felt a sense of hopelessness from everyone working that night. This feeling wasn't from a life lost or any incident in the ER. This was like a dream, except it was actually happening.

I distinctly remember the negative chatter of marriages falling apart, moms working their fourth & fifth extra shift that week away from family to pay the bills, kids staying with neighbors, and friends supporting their families solely because of divorce or other reasons. There was a lot of loneliness felt that we didn't even have to talk about it.

Caring for others in healthcare is very hard and the lifestyle often leaves little motivation for the caregivers to care for themselves. Many are unfulfilled and so they believe there is no other way and find no balance at the expense of their families and themselves. I was even told once, "You knew what you were getting into, you were called to this and you should have known that this would be your life."

That night, I realized that I, too, was beginning to live like everyone else. I was saying the exact same things and feeling the exact same way. I wasn't able to be present at home, physically and mentally, my marriage was an afterthought, I had developed an uncontrollable coping mechanism of anxiety and a pattern of not sleeping trying to be "better," to be "more" and "do more" to make myself feel better.

I had never felt so trapped, felt so lost. I felt controlled by something that I couldn't control.

I remember one of the hardest things was feeling so ashamed that I was miserable, earning a great income, somewhat enjoyed my role in helping others and fixing problems, but feeling so miserably empty!

Am I supposed to just live like this?
Why do I feel so lost and empty?

And I will never forget, in the midst of all the darkness, a little voice that I had heard many times before gently whispered, "I love you! I haven't forgotten about you! If you would just spend some quality time with me, I have been trying to help you! And by the way, YOU ARE NOT LIKE EVERYONE ELSE. You do not need to copy the behaviors and customs of the world! You do not have to stay miserable, you do not have to live a life like that. As a matter of fact, I need you to be the light for ME." I know this was the Holy Spirit speaking to me.

But I was lost and felt trapped. I felt as though I could no longer be myself and I was questioning who I was. Yet my heart longed to make a difference, to serve others, to impact the world. But I had no idea where to start, what to do? What do we do when the rubber meets the road? When one arm is being pulled one way to stay comfortable, but your other arm is being pulled to make a change?

This is where you can choose to fill your own gap or let JESUS be EVERYTHING! For me, there was no denying that my circumstances and the way things were working out were guiding me down another road in my journey, and it was time to listen to the voice of the Holy Spirit and make a change.

I wasn't even sure where to start.

But I started.

I need you to understand, I was a mess. So much was on my plate, I had so many insecurities, and I was concerned that nothing would change. I felt so lost, but there was something in me, the spirit in me was still alive. Although I felt isolated and forgotten, the spirit never left. The little light had been flickering all along. It was alive; I was just keeping it covered up.

So this dark place made me realize that even though I wasn't sure how to be or what to do, I could still move forward. I believed that things were supposed to be different. I BELIEVED.

Maybe you feel lost and confused and unsure. Maybe you feel that you have nothing in you to even try.

I get it, I understand.

But I want you to know that I am not giving up on you and God certainly has not or you would not be here reading this book. Hello!! Remember when I said he would keep throwing things at you until you saw it, felt it, and until you realized that he is trying to help you?

Hot Mess Momma. THIS IS YOUR SIGN.

Here is what Paul says in Romans 12:1-2:

No More Hot Mess Mantra:

I am a new creation-

Romans 12:1-2

So here's what I want you to do, God helping you: Take your everyday, ordinary life—your sleeping, eating, going-to-work, and walking-around life—and place it before God as an offering. Embracing what God does for you is the best thing you can do for him. Don't become so well-adjusted to your culture that you fit into it without even thinking. Instead, fix your attention on God. You'll be changed from the inside out. Readily recognize what he wants from you, and quickly respond to it. Unlike the culture around you, always dragging you down to its level of immaturity, God brings the best out of you, develops well-formed maturity in you. (The Message Bible)

Take your life, all of it, and offer it to God! All the comfortable things, all the hard things, all the good things, all the things that you know God is telling you he wants you to do, and all the things he's telling to quit doing... GIVE THEM UP!

He continues to say, "embracing what God does for you is the best thing you can do for him."

- Be open and willing to do what he is telling you to do: stay or move
- Even if it's hard, even if it doesn't make sense, even if it's scary or really uncomfortable

(God already knew what we would be thinking because he inspired Paul to send us this message.)

Don't become so well-adjusted to your culture that you fit into it without even thinking. He already knows we want to leave our marriages, he already knows we don't want to volunteer, he already knows we don't want to get up early to spend time with him or to eat healthy or exercise.

I think about my job situation, which would ultimately be a HUGE life transformation for me, and looking back, it had very little to do with my job and EVERYTHING to do with ME. My situation was based on where I was personally and my relationship with God. I needed HIM. I had distanced myself from Him and he was simply getting my attention. It was painful, it was hard, but I had done enough striving and enough working hard to feel better about myself. Jesus was literally kicking down walls and meeting me in the dark hallways saying, "I have a better plan for you if you will just come sit and chat with me for a while. Let me show you WHO YOU ARE AND WHOSE YOU ARE!" (Jeremiah

29:11; Psalm 46:10; Isaiah 43:1) When you are walking with Him, unlike the culture around you always dragging you down to its level of immaturity, God brings the best out of you and develops well-formed maturity in you. The only way to understand ourselves is by what God is and by what he does for us, not by what we are and what we do for him.

Think about Paul who wrote Romans. The writing of the book took place about 30 years after the life, death, and resurrection of Jesus. This was a letter written by Paul to the Romans. When Paul wrote it, he was an ordinary guy. He was nothing special except he was astounded by the life of Christ and wanted to understand what it meant. He passionately pursued his understanding of Jesus and then passionately, with conviction and inspiration by the Holy Spirit, he wrote about it. What I find so remarkable is not only the book of Romans and the truth it gives, but also that Paul was an ordinary guy that passionately pursued Christ and wrote a letter that later became the premier document of Christian theology. God used this ordinary man, his gifts, and something he believed in so passionately to literally change the world.

Despite all that he went through, what others thought of him, what the outcome would be, he BELIEVED. And because of this belief, he did.

How do we get here, to a place of sacrificial action deeply rooted in belief?

You start. Whether you want to or not. You start.

#NoMoreHotMess

Chapter 3

When I was in such a dark and confusing place, when I finally looked to Him for help and for guidance, here's what I found:

o He was there with me! He had not gone anywhere. (Jeremiah 29:13) All I needed to do was look. I had to make intentional efforts in the midst of my mess to look for Jesus. What is Jesus doing right now in your life? Take a second and think about something good He is doing right now and write it below.

_____
_____
_____
_____
_____
_____
_____

o Back when I was a new momma who worked rotating shifts in the ER, I usually had to get up early enough before my shift to start looking at Scripture and write out my affirmations. It had to be simple, because Lord knew I couldn't handle much. I believed that I could make the time and that this habit truly mattered. So, I did. I started in the only place that I knew to find bright, colorful, engaging ideas, organized plans, and things. Pinterest. I typed in "Scripture reading plan." Lots came up. I knew I needed a plan because I knew I couldn't think much. I just needed to be able to open up the plan and easily find what I needed to do. I found a bright and colorful "anxiety" themed plan, got a blank piece of paper, and started writing the one Scripture it recommended. A few months later, I decided that I wanted to start creating my own calendars. It was fun and made me feel a little more invested in the process, plus it was something I could share with you! It is so so simple but so so powerful to get you to start simply connecting with your heavenly daddy each day.

Go to cheneiltorbert.com now, and in our shop you can grab a calendar and some free weekly updates from me, along with recipes, tips, and upcoming events.

o Soon after starting to write down Scripture, I realized that a huge missing link for me in the mess was that I had stopped looking for good. My pessimistic nature is always looking for the worst in myself and situations, so that's what I was doing: focusing on the negative. So I started intentionally writing gratitude daily, being grateful for what God was already doing instead of focusing on all of my inadequacies and what wasn't happening in life. Focus on what is good and acknowledge my gratitude tangibly. I bet you can make a list of good stuff that you are grateful for, too.

There are tons of fancy ways to do this, but all you need is the same piece of paper that you write your Scripture and affirmations on and then just number three things, different things, you are thankful for every day. If you want to be intentional in your marriage, tell your husband that you are going to write some love notes to him every day on the mirror, whiteboard, or little notebook in your bathroom. Then tell him you would really appreciate if he would return the favor. Do not do what I did and spend 30 days writing lovely notes without telling him your expectation. Trust me, this will prevent you from becoming a bitter mess thinking you are unloved and unappreciated because you assumed that he would just return the messages.

In the space below, write out the date that you will commit to adding daily gratitude to your morning quiet time and then spend a few minutes writing down some ideas that you think you would enjoy and that your husband or kids might appreciate. Then write down the date you will commit to start doing the intentional acts of love and kindness.

_____
_____
_____
_____
_____
_____
_____
_____
_____
_____
_____
_____
_____

Chapter 3

Chapter 4

Safe and Secure and an Irrational Mess

I am secure in God's love and His Power

Let perseverance finish its work so that you may be mature and complete, not lacking anything (James 1:4)

"MOM!!!" my son yelled.

"Remember, I am supposed to bring a shape. Remember, I was telling you yesterday that we learned about a circle, square, rectangle, triangle, and I have to bring one of these shapes TODAY!" Of course, I had to ask him to repeat himself several times because me, Mrs. Hotmess Express, had just finished up a video in my bathroom sharing my heart with you, and I was distracted. My mind was all over the place. Not to mention it was already five minutes past time to leave, I was trying to hide the smell with my favorite bath and body lotion since I didn't have to time to shower (so please tell me if it is not working next time you see me), and I was quickly applying my 24-hour non-smudge lipstick to make myself feel like I at least look presentable since I had no time for makeup as he rounds the corner in tears.

"MOM!!!! I can't find the shape. You know the one I was telling you about yesterday, in the car ride home, while you were trying to calm brother down as he was screaming

55

uncontrollably in his car seat?" That's what I heard anyways…

"You mean literally the very LAST minute before we are late for school you need me to find the nonexistent shape somewhere in this house?"

Trying to compose myself before raising my voice, which is very difficult for me, I frantically looked at my lifesaving husband who always comes to the rescue when myself or my kids decide to open a can of crazy at the last minute. As I am looking at my five-year-old, who is about to cry, (but I can tell is also confident that we won't let him down) daddy the hero finds a hexagon magnet at the bottom of the toy chest just before I blurt out some really unkind words about his teacher asking for such a ridiculous request from the parents of a five-year-old kindergartener. Because we all know who has to do all of these things, right? But I withheld my words because at this point, I think it was my son who was confused about what was needed. I didn't want to be that mom who doesn't send the requested work back to school. Although we never even got that request, but anyways, oh that morning was not too different than many others with this #hotmessexpress.

We celebrated and hugged and yes, inevitably pulled into the car line at 8:00 am when he was supposed to be sitting in his class. As the teacher was helping him out of the car, she kindly reminded me that as of tomorrow we would have to park and I would have to check him in the office from here on out if he was here at 8. So me, already in full-on hotness mentality mode, heard her say, "Cheneil, you are a bad mom and because you are late, you will cause your child to have a consequence since you are not on time. His punctuality ultimately affects the other facility, volunteers, his class, and teacher. You should do better."

And you know what I wanted to do with the magnet that made us late because at that point I was more of an #irrationalhotmess.

And yes girl, you guessed it, when I picked him up, he indeed said he was confused about when the shape was due. I still don't know if it was the ridiculous shape request or the day we were supposed to bring it, but y'all, I could have choked that precious child of mine. I was annoyed, but I understood. I mean there must be rules and start times and end times and projects for learning. There must be, this is REAL LIFE. The one we all live and experience on a daily basis.

I am 100% sure we were not the only parents who were frantically trying to get our child EXACTLY what he/she needed and sacrificing lots of our own things and agendas to make sure it happens. Sports, after-school activities, projects… the list could go on. We sacrifice A LOT for others, don't we?

When was the last time you committed to do something that was uncomfortable for your kids, your spouse, your parents, a friend? The last time you did something that required extra effort that was a bit inconvenient or uncomfortable? We have ALL been there. But can I ask you an honest question, sister?

When was the last time this person was YOU?

When was the last time you made sacrifices for yourself? You made yourself a priority? You got uncomfortable and did that thing you know you need to do or have been wanting to do because you knew there was a positive impact it would make? When was the last time you went above and beyond to make sure you were growing, learning, seeking to understand, or remind yourself just how loved and precious you are?

When was the last time you looked at yourself and your life and said, "God cares just as much about me as I do for others. And Yes, I AM WORTHY AND WORTH IT TOO"? Can you remember? I already know what's going on in your head sister, so let's talk this through a bit…

I don't have time for me, are you crazy. It's a rat race around here.

- Time – love, what are you making time for? You have 45 minutes to an hour that you can use to improve your life each day. Even when working 13-hour shifts I could listen to an audiobook on the way to work or take the stairs. I could pack healthier food, I could even get in a quick 30-minute workout before work. What you do have is time. We all do. You are just choosing to do other things with your time. Things that do not impact your future positively.

I am actually OK just how I am and believe God is OK with that, too, although, secretly I can't quit thinking about taking the leap into using my gifts in another way. Doing something different is scary and I am ok with being comfortable.

- Dreams – You are already halfway there. Do you hear yourself? God has already put something in your heart, sister. You are thinking about something, but you are pretending that you aren't. You have told yourself there must be more and there IS MORE. Yes, it will require time and effort. Yes, it will be hard and yes, it is easier to just clock in and work for someone else, but sister. If God is putting a dream on your heart, then you have to go for it. Don't miss out on his gift to you.

And Cheneil, I believe that God knows that my kids have to be a priority over myself, but I can barely get down and play with them and I just don't feel good most of the time, which impacts my mood so I know things need to change, but they matter most right now.

- Health – Ok, you know what, your kids do matter, a lot. Your kids deserve a healthy mother, because our health is the one thing that we all need to live this life. And can you be completely involved and active in their life being unhealthy, possibly, but I want better for you. I do not want my own kids to look at another mother as an example of how to live life. Yes, they need mentors and others to look up to, but I count it as a privilege to be the best example I know how. I will make mistakes, lots of them, because that's real life, but I plan to come back and show them that I am trying to be the best example I can, show them what I would want them to do.

Girl, I work a full-time job, my kids have activities, my husband doesn't help much, so making time for me is not even a possibility. But if I am being honest, most nights when I am binge watching This is Us for about

2 hours each night, I do feel a little guilty and even think about doing some squats or crunches during commercials, especially if I see an insanity commercial or something. But then realize, NETFLIX, hello, has no commercials, plus I work so hard and I feel I deserve this time.

- Downtime – Oh yes, yes, yes, you deserve some downtime. But when TV for 2 hours each day becomes the reason that you cannot make time for yourself, sister, I love you, but this is not OK. Your TV watching is now a problem.

And Cheneil, I love you, but I don't get to work from home coaching others and sitting around writing books like you. My job requires so much time and energy, it requires that I leave early, and by the time I get home, I just can't. I mean, I sometimes feel like I could maybe go for a walk on my lunch break or walk with the kids. You know, now that I think about it, sometimes I even wake up before my alarm and know I need to read your devotion Cheneil, but I feel I need to find motivation from the Facebook group and I usually end up just laying in bed scrolling. I have to think all day, so this is "my time." I do this in the evening, too. And I am OK with this because when God is ready, he will help me do what I need to do.

- Personal/Spiritual Growth – LOVE, you are in control. YOU! Every single person has the exact number of hours in the day. You have heard this before. I know you have. And about comparison. Who cares what other people are doing. And do you really know they have more time than you? The reality is, you are not OK with the way that you are living your life. And you are the only one who can change that. It's time to stop rationalizing your inaction and do something. Do the best you can today. God has already told you to take action and that he would help. There is no better time, there is no more time. The best time is NOW. YOU deserve now.

I am so tired and frankly, I don't want to do anything different. I just can't. I remember when I felt the best. I was getting up a little earlier and exercising before work. It always gave me a different energy and better attitude and I ate better too, but I just don't have the motivation. Cheneil, you don't understand. I just can't. I want to, but I am waiting on God to help me.

My husband does not support me in living a healthy lifestyle. This makes it very difficult for me. I have all the tools I need, I know what to do, but I just can't seem to be motivated enough to do anything. I remember a few years ago when I was more focused on making time for reading and writing Scripture or a simple devotion in the morning and especially writing out a few things I am thankful for. I was in a better mood and had more grace towards my husband. Even felt like his lack of support didn't bother me as much since I was so focused myself and he actually started to make a few changes too, then. But wait, he is just not going to support me in this, so the timing is just not right. Forget it.

- Support – You do not need anyone's support or anyone's approval to live your best life. PERIOD. Yes, it helps if you have support, but if you are waiting for the support you need for YOU to take action on whatever it is that you need to do, then you are not only putting a ridiculous expectation on that person, but you are also using them as your excuse. Yes, excuse. You need to do you and work towards your best you. For YEARS my husband has not been on the same page as me with many things. Health being a huge one. If I would have waited on his support, I would be living a completely different life, not just physically, but emotionally and spiritually. I have grown because I choose to do what I can do despite the support or approval anyone gives me.

- I will have to answer for me and what I did here on earth and I want to be physically, emotionally, and spiritually ready and available to do anything the Lord asks of me.
- You will have to answer for you, not your husband.

I can't even think straight, Cheneil, so trying to fit "ME" in is just not possible. My laundry, my house, the kids and their needs, all the things I have on my plate, take up all of my extra energy so I have none left to give. I know that when I actually make a little time for me, I have more energy. I know this and remember this, but I need a group of people to hold me accountable, and right now that is not an option. So for now, I will just wait for a better time.

- Motivation – Other people cannot motivate you. I know that it seems like when you are part of a group or community that you are more motivated, but I have been actively involved in both physical classes as well as virtual classes and I have convinced myself that I cannot do anything at home or online. It won't work or be as effective. And it all comes down to your mindset. You either want to change or you don't, and you are either willing to do what it takes or you aren't. Motivation is simply your mindset. I am not here to persuade you to get healthy any certain way, although I am passionate about my virtual training groups because they have been the most effective for me. But what I do know is it does not matter where you go or often even what you do if you do not have the right mindset.

- You cannot continue to use the excuse of your mess, time, energy, and people as the reason why you cannot do what you know you need to do. Your plate will always be full and there will never be a "right time."

Honestly, I don't think God really cares too much about my healthy lifestyle. I mean, as long as I am kind and caring of others and am a good person, then I think he is OK, so I will be OK. I often feel a little thing telling me I should maybe consider getting a little more active just for the emotional and cardiovascular benefits, I know that's the right thing, but I am not sick or needing medication right now. God is going to help me be OK.

Helping myself requires money and we don't have any. I have to get my nails redone every two weeks, my kids have two sports they are playing right now, and usually we have to eat out several times a week because of our busy schedule, so money is going to be a problem. I mean I know that if I put a hold on a few of their sports, we wouldn't be gone as much and we would save a little. And if we weren't gone as much we wouldn't have to eat out as much and would save some and maybe I would have the money. But… the kids. I just feel they are more important than me right now. I need to do something, but they matter more.

I have been begging God to show up and help me, but I have decided that God will help me when he is ready and until he physically moves me or slaps the cookie out of my hand, I am taking it that it's OK.

We've all said them.

If you are in Jesus, then I know you have felt a prompting for change at some point in your life. (2 Corinthians 5:17) God is going to constantly be drawing us closer to Him, showing us something new, and guiding our next steps, if we are willing. The Holy Spirit wants to be our guide.

Most often, when we feel this prompting or nudge to make some positive changes in our lives that require us to make ourselves a priority, we automatically pull the red flag and start thinking of all the reason why we shouldn't, why we can't, or flat our dig our heels in and decide we don't want to. We instantly convince ourselves that we are NOT worthy or worth it.

Remember the shape we had to find for my son? What if you said all of these things above to your child who was frantically asking you to find a non-existent object, in what seemed to be an impossible amount of time, while he is standing there looking at you with an expectant heart?

What if you said, "I don't have time, I don't think you are that important and I don't think you are worthy enough for me to put out that effort for you."? Somewhere along the road, you decided, we decided, that we are not worthy of goodness, greatness, and the vast grace-filled promises of our heavenly daddy. Somewhere along the way, we deemed ourselves unworthy, undeserving. Therefore, we find ourselves living in a place of false beliefs that we have made our truth.

Through series of events from our past, through personal failures, through the things we were told or were not told as we grew older, or simply the deceitful and intentional acts of the devil himself… in all the mess of life, we limit ourselves and take ownership of our busy, messy lives as our identity. We decide that we ARE a mess and it has become our identity and we have allowed ourselves to live in this place of safety because we simply don't believe that we deserve better or that God created us for anything more. Or maybe we just don't think we are worthy of anything more.

But let me tell you dear and beloved sister:

You are so much more than your HOTMESS, your circumstance, your past, your struggles. When you said YES to Jesus, you said YES to removal of all sin, all shame, all chains, all of the mess (Isaiah 1:18; 1 John 1:7). He took it to the cross with Him! He knew long ago that we were going to be a hotmess. He knew what struggles we would have and he loves YOU so much that he said, "You know what, I will send my son to die for you and all of your hotmess. Because I love you that much. I want you to live in freedom, in peace." God's greatest desire through the death and resurrection of Jesus is that we feel secure in his unconditional love and vast power. To truly KNOW Him. That's what God says! His death was our way to FREEDOM.

He loves you and that is why he is pointing you in certain directions. He cares and is guiding you. Even though sometimes it does not make sense and we feel the need to see the reason, the how, the why, His desire is that we understand Him so well and trust Him so much that we don't question, we just trust. Be so in tune with His ways that we don't doubt. And this is difficult. I get it. It takes willingness, an open mind and heart, and trust.

> ### No More Hot Mess Mantra:
>
> I am secure in God's love and in His power.
>
> Romans 8:38-39

If you find yourself having a hard time grasping His love or understanding how anyone could care so much about our decisions in this life, our peace in this life, please know you are not alone. As a matter of fact, you are in the right place.

I lived the ultimate self-sufficient life for so long. And I am addicted, so this is an ongoing battle for me. I want to do all and be all. I was in disbelief of God's love for me, so I tried to earn it. I have also been in a state of exhaustion and felt like I have nothing left to give. Quite frankly I felt nothing, indifferent, and didn't want to do anything.

And guess what, God found me. He has met me everywhere I have been. And I believe that is why you are holding this book. God is meeting you where you are and wants to show you that you are worth it.

You are WORTH so much, even dying for.

No More Mess:

- Your past or current circumstances have likely shaped your subconscious view of yourself. For years I wasn't even aware that I was telling myself that I was not worthy and that even when I would accomplish things, it wasn't good enough. The enemy started deceiving me at an early age. So you might be telling yourself things like "I can never, I won't ever, I am not," before you even realize, like I was doing. Can you think of a situation right now, a thing that maybe you feel in your heart you need to do, but you have subconsciously said, "I can never, I won't ever, I am not"?

- Can you fill in the blanks?

    o   I will never

    _____

    _____

    _____

    _____

    _____

    o   I won't ever

    _____

    _____

    _____

    _____

    _____

    _____

- One of the most empowering things that I have been taught are affirmations. At first, I thought they were a bit corny and well, "not something I needed" or had time for. But, if you have been following me for a bit, you know affirming God's truth has become the cornerstone of where I am today and the changes that God has been wanting me to make. They have become my belief system instead of all the lies that I was telling myself for so long. I had to learn His truth and believe it. Below, write the #nomorehotmess affirmation and Scripture (I am secure in God's love and in His power. Romans 8:38-39) followed by an I CAN and I WILL statement. Share how this truth makes you feel empowered to live differently.

_____

_____

_____

_____

_____

_____

_____

_____

_____

_____

_____

_____

_____

_____

_____

_____

_____

_____

Chapter 5

The Messy Mentality

My Mess will be Miracle

James 1:2-5

After I had been a nurse for about a year, I soon realized that I started to feel like I was "just a nurse." A number among many brilliant, selfless, amazing men and women. It is an amazing job and the impact you can have is truly amazing, but for some reason, I felt like I was just a number, like I was no different than the other amazing nurses I now called my medical family. I mean, heavens, we literally spent days, nights, weekends, and holidays together, more time together than with our own families by far. But I could not help but feel like a number.

You see, long before I was born, God put this desire in my heart to make a difference, to leave an imprint on this earth. I can't explain this in entirety other than it is in my spirit and I feel like I have been on the pursuit of this for a long time. I have been trying to understand this and well, in true Cheneil fashion, forcing my way, working my way, using my own might and bullheaded personality into figuring it out. Anyone else feel like you have this God-given gift of gusto about life, ambition for feeling needed and wanted?

Before college, I honestly didn't know what I wanted to do, but I felt this desire to serve and help and through an encounter at a dermatologist's office. I was literally astounded by the nurses' knowledge and skill and kindness towards me. I don't know if it was because I had felt so ashamed and embarrassed that I was a sophomore in college and had acne like a 13-year-old and she helped me feel less embarrassed, or if this was a divine encounter that the Lord was showing me as an opportunity that I could maybe do one day. I will never forget that encounter that day.

I left thinking two things:

#1: I would love to do that, to be an expert, to be viewed as "smart" because I had never felt smart. I always struggled with comprehension, school, and test-taking in particular. But something in my inner being said, "You can do that. No, you may not be as smart as most, but you have a hustle and drive that could outwork anyone." So, I literally remember thinking, "I want to prove to myself that against intellectual odds, I can do that."

#2: I want to leave a lasting impression on people. When people come in contact with me, I want to empower them in love and truth to take action. (Ephesians 4:15) She empowered me. Now clearly, I was at a dermatologist office, not a Joyce Myers revival, but something happened in my 23-year-old heart that honestly I have not been able to put words behind until today.

I look back on this now that I am no longer practicing medicine full-time and think to myself, "Thank you, Jesus, for that nurse and that experience, because I went on to be a nurse practitioner." Little did I know that that was merely a stepping stone in God's plans for me, but I am so thankful for all of the hardship and people and opportunities that all started in that dermatologist's office in Longview, Texas.

Honestly, I never imagined I could even become a nurse because I was not smart enough to do that. But then it became a pursuit of making myself feel worthy and good enough, and you better be darn sure that I went for it.

My career as a nurse practitioner, on a personal level, was purely out of a deep, deep desire to be enough. I had a desire to feel needed, wanted, to feel smart enough, and despite the mess of a person I had decided I was, to prove that I was capable and hope that my family and God himself would be proud of me and pour his favor into my life. And the saga continued. It wasn't until ten years into medicine, after finally bargaining, praying, having my first child, and "agreeing with God" that maybe I am capable of being a mother that I finally saw what I had done.

I enjoyed my job as someone who cared for the sick. It is an amazing job. But my career was about position. It was about doing more and more to create a false identity. My work, the accolades, the income, had become my identity. I can truthfully say that this was not my intent, it was not done on purpose, but what I had done was misplaced my identity and my worth on my performance. If I did more, God would be proud. If I didn't, he would be disappointed and withhold favor.

Getting a degree was super hard for me, but it meant that I was proving I am capable, I am worthy, and I am enough. Looking back, obviously God had a HUGE role in my eight years of education and 14 years at the bedside caring for sick children. And that path for me was exactly where I needed to be and what I needed to be doing. God was preparing my heart, my mind, thickening my skin, and he would break and rebuild my spirit so that I could truly LIVE. I had so many amazing people and opportunities and chances for God to be the light through me. All of this is so good, and life felt great. As I mentioned before, with the nice home, the luxury car, the money, the vacations, living life on my terms was pretty darn good. It was tiring, but manageable and controllable.

And then LIFE happened. My little gift from above, Tatum, came, and boy was I in for a crazy ride. Loss of control happened. I didn't recognize it at first and I tried to fight it. I needed control. I was used to control so I desperately tried to find it wherever I could. Pregnancy was great except I couldn't control my body or what was happening. Obviously, I had to get over that real quick, so I then tried to find something else. My husband was in the middle of a career change and ended up staying home with our boys because well, I could control things better.

And then I had my son. If you are a mother, you know that control is impossible. And y'all, when I say I was a mess, please hear me… I WAS A MESS. On every level, in every way. I showed up to work after three months of maternity leave "ready to be the hands and feet of God" and it was horrible. I was not who I thought I was. I was no longer strong enough to have no sleep and still work. I was no longer capable of being all things to all people and be the positive light I once was. And oh boy did I try, and did a lot of fake it till you… well for me… not make it.

I just kept showing up, pushing my limits and myself like I was supposed to and honestly, doing what I only knew how to do: work harder. I hoped God would see me, find favor with me, and I could start feeling more in control again. My work and desire to fix things created an even bigger mess. Because you know what happens when we work hard, believe we are doing good and trying to earn God's favor, and nothing happens... the lies start coming. The enemy loves to catch us when we are exhausted and feeling less than, and throw curve balls ninety to nothing, like the balls coming from one of those pitching machines. You know what I am talking about; when you are standing in the batting cages and the balls just start coming, you aren't ready, you miss ball after ball, and then one hits you.

Picture it: just like the balls, the enemy loves to throw these thoughts when we aren't ready and when we least expect it, so that we feel out of control, helpless, lost, and YES, like a total mess.

You are not capable. You are not worthy of a happy home. No, he does not love you and you deserve better. You do not deserve to stay at home with your kids. Your kids don't deserve you. You are not a good mother. You have created this mess and you are being punished. No, your husband is not attracted to you anymore because you are lazy and have let yourself go. No, there is no way out of this and now you have to sit in misery. YES YOU ARE A MESS. That is who you are, who you have always been and yep, you got it right, that is who you probably always will be.

The lies. And the enemy wants nothing more than to keep you here. Keep me here. To keep us here.

Think about this last week: the chaos, the mess, the overwhelming. What if your neighbor needed help? What if your husband needed extra attention? What if a friend needed some encouragement? What about you? What have you done for YOU to fill your cup this past week?

Just writing this makes me think of a new neighbor that moved into our neighborhood. She was a stay-at-home mom of a two-year-old whose husband was away at work most of the day. He had mentioned to my husband they were new to the area and his wife was at home and my husband even told me. But y'all, I was so sucked into my issues, my feelings of being overwhelmed, my stress, my HOTMESS that I didn't even think about how lonely she must have been. It was weeks after I had finally allowed the Lord to take control of my mess that I clued into my responsibility as a daughter of Jesus to make sure she knew she was noticed and cared for. Yes, this is something I should do.

No More Hot Mess Mantra:
I am unselfish-
Philippians 2:3

My husband. Your husband. Yes, they have needs too. (Philippians 2:3) And as often as I ignore them because I feel like mine aren't being met, that doesn't make his any less significant. They need attention, too. But I know for myself, I get so bogged down by the to-do list, the kid's needs, the mess, that I overlook when I need a loving thank you, or I appreciate you, I notice you, a hug, a hand held... I go from distracted by LIFE, to then needy, to then bitter, to then forget you. But he has needs, too.

And as hurtful as it is to write, I can find myself so selfish and needy in my marriage that I often expect more than I am willing to dish out. I place my emotional mess at a higher priority than my husband's at times, and this is exactly what the enemy wants. Think about it. When we care more about our needs than others, they can never do anything right. They cannot measure up, and because of this, we allow ourselves to back away and don't even look for what they need. They become not good enough, we become incompatible. Doubt and lies are planted or keep sprouting.

The enemy wants us so distracted and uneasy that we never feel well-loved, enough, at peace, or complete. Or he wants us to look to the wrong places to mend these hurts. He wants nothing more than to give us a MESSY MENTALITY and make us believe that it is who we are and then make us comfortable with this. The enemy wants us content with the mess so that we cannot hear from God, think clearly, and you guessed it… NOT LIVE OUT OUR PURPOSE. He wants us to not be the light, not share Jesus, and NOT DO WHAT WE WERE CREATED TO DO.

The enemy knows that if we focus on our mess or our struggles that we can't seem to overcome, our failures that we can't seem to forgive ourselves from or move past, and our shortcomings, we stay distracted. The enemy is also really good at making us compare ourselves to others, even by the everyday stuff, like the two-week-old pile of laundry or crayon marks on the wall, the scum in the bathroom shower, or the yard or house that isn't quite as nice or seem as welcoming. Or what about those of us who say we function better in the mess, the "organized chaos," but then find ourselves constantly on edge or anxious, even empty?

When we constantly focus on our mess, we start to believe that we ARE a mess.

This becomes our character, our identity, doesn't it?

This happened to me. It was not a place I had found myself before. NOT that I haven't been there before many times and created tons of messes in my life, but my recent encounter with Mrs. HotMessExpress left a mark. It was different. It hit me like a ton of bricks. For several weeks in a row I hit snooze and neglected my morning routine, which was a HUGE red flag for me since this is my MOMMA time and Jesus time, something I do even when on vacation. I am a crazy mess without this time.

So when I didn't get up, that meant no intentional, sacrificial, focused Jesus for several weeks. During this hotmess express detour, I had also told myself that I didn't have anything to write in this book. I had allowed lots of unnecessary sugary treats into my hands and mouth, leaving me in pain, feeling bloated, and body shaming myself. I had started neglecting my husband out of selfishness because I had felt so bad about myself. I had neglected others in my life when I could have used a friend. My mind was in shambles and I had accepted the #hotmess mentality as who I really was. And the enemy was working to convince me that that is actually who I always was. And for a second, I felt like this was OK. I mean, the shirts were cute. I had already told y'all that I bought the coffee mugs and I felt like maybe I would be more likable and relatable if I was a self-proclaimed glorified hotmess like so many were preaching.

The enemy was making me believe that because I had lots of mess going on in my life and I had let a lot of areas in my life get real messy, I was indeed too far gone and was officially too messy to do much of anything beyond surviving the days. My future was basically made up. The devil started to plant little seeds of doubt in my head and heart about my entire dream. God's request for me to speak, coach, have a ranch to minister to people, adopt, and lead medical missions were attacked by different schemes of the devil that would make me question my very existence on earth.

I became so upset with myself that I was having trouble enjoying my boys. My oldest would be starting Kindergarten and I couldn't even let myself enjoy him some days because I was so concerned with what I was doing wrong and why the Lord was just watching all of this happen. So, of course, this would give the enemy more ammunition. And I was surviving. I was just going through the motions, trying to keep up, trying to enjoy life and my boys and yes, yummy food. The living was supposed to be easy. WRONG.

This was one of many times in my life that I know the Lord gave me the heart to serve others and bring others into community. He knew that throughout my life that I would need accountability, and often I am so stubborn that I do not ask for help or prayer. So, he showed me the opportunity to coach others in their lifestyle journey, and as a coach I show up, not because I have to, but because I want to. I want to be there as an example and to help these ladies propel forward in life. So even when I don't feel like it, I have others depending on me to show up, so I do. This is a glorious built-in system that I am forever grateful for. You should join us!

But I kept showing up for these ladies, I was reading Scripture, I was working out, and eating healthy food. Even when I didn't want to, I was. And even though for many days I did not feel like I was hearing from God, he steadily, in grace and love, kept pursuing me. He saw me. He was pursuing me and wanting to help me.

Just like he sees you, sister. He has not left you. He will never leave us.

He had an assignment for me, just like he does for you, and he was going to keep pursuing me until he got my attention. On the mornings that I was allowing Jesus to be a part of my day, He was constantly reminding me of His love and His truth. Through my kids, my husband, mentor, friends, my parents, and women I was coaching.

I would read my affirmations in the mornings.

You are capable. You are strong. You are a beautiful masterpiece. You are worthy. You have God's power in you. You are disciplined. Literally I was reading Miracles in the Mess most mornings, and I was reminded of who I really was. But y'all, I wasn't listening, like so many of you. We have gotten ourselves in such a MESS. It is not that he isn't present, but we have allowed ourselves to believe he isn't here because we are literally covering Him up, pushing him away, and choosing our mess.

Am I right?

Listen to me! Your life might be a mess. Who's isn't. But you are NOT a mess.

No More Hot Mess Mantra:

I am a LOVED, beautiful, forgiven, redeemed, unique, precious masterpiece-

---

Your truth is that:

You are LOVED (Jeremiah 31:3).

You are a beautiful (Proverbs 31:30).

You are forgiven (1 John 1:7-9).

You are redeemed (1 John 4:4).

You are unique (Romans 12:6).

You are a precious masterpiece that the Lord God himself hand-crafted with unique qualities and gifts (Isaiah 43:1).

He loves you so much that he has asked you to partner with Him using your gifts. Does that mean that our lives are not going to get messy? UMMM... of course not. Does that mean we are not going to feel like we are a mess most of the time? UMMM... no! Because we all do.

But sister, YOU ARE NOT A MESS. That is not who you are.

So please stop accepting hotmess as a badge of honor. I can assure you that when we do, the enemy will use this as ammunition to fuel all of our insecurities, doubts, shortcomings and ultimately our identity. He will do everything he can to replace our gift of FREEDOM for HOTMESS, and sister, you are worth so much more than a mess.

Let me be honest. When the Lord asked me to write this book based around self-discipline and not identifying with the oh-so-glorified #hotmess mentality, I cringed. I literally thought, "Are you kidding me. I already feel like people roll their eyes at me, shame me, and even hurt me because I have been told I am unrelatable." I did not want to go here. I didn't want to make myself more uncomfortable or insecure in some ways, and I did not want to make anyone else feel bad like I had been made to feel I had done many times before.

But here I am, allowing the Lord to share through me. Not because it is easy, but because this is not about me. *This is about our identity in Christ.* It is about swapping the messy mentality for a kingdom mentality, for a mentality of truth. You were created to be disciplined in all areas of your life. (2 Timothy 1:7) Despite our wiring, our personalities, our past, we ARE disciplined.

I have found self-discipline to be something I feel empowered by. It is part of our NEW creation, our new character, after we have received Jesus. (2 Corinthians 5:17) Just all of the fruits of the spirit; patience, gentleness, kindness. (Galatians 5:22-23) We ALL have them in us. I know what you are thinking. "UMMM, Cheneil, my apple seed must have fallen from a different tree. I am not and have never seen myself as disciplined." Or maybe you are thinking, "Yep, I can handle the house and get to work on time, but my health, nope, not disciplined." Or, "Yep, when it comes to my kids, their activities, or school, I can get them up, make lunches, and get everyone out on time, but I know my marriage needs work and my husband needs attention. But I just can't." Or, "The debt, that has accumulated is quite choking and I want to give more, but I just can't seem to stick to the Money Makeover plan we committed to. So you say God made us all disciplined, I am not sure I believe."

I get it. Truly, I do! The Lord has been asking me to write this book for months and somehow, "I" was not disciplined enough to make it happen.

But the truth is, discipline is not about SELF at all.

Discipline is about belief, believing in God and His power, and out of that belief we walk in this belief as being obedient. We are obedient because we believe God is able. It is about doing the right thing when it doesn't make sense, when it doesn't seem to matter, when its hard, and uncomfortable. We do it because we believe that our actions, our efforts, our impact, and our obedience really does matter.

What if this stuff, all the things that keep coming back to tug at your heart, the things that keep overwhelming you, the things that keep bringing stress or anxiety, the difficulties we face, is God pulling you in closer to him. I don't care if it's about you sticking to a diet change, or your marriage, or money stuff. Y'all, it all matters, and God wants to help you with it all. And what if how you are feeling is exactly what you need to be feeling so that you actually understand that it's time to make a change? A heart and mind change. Your mentality dictates your life. What you think about, you bring about. You have to make a shift from being a hotmess to being a WHOLE, COMPLETE, NEW CREATION IN CHRIST (2 CORINTHIANS 5:17). You have to grow in this deep belief of love that your heavenly daddy has for you and what he thinks of you. You have to believe that you matter so much to Him that he wants to partner with you in this messy life. And until you change your mentality, you can't fully do that.

No More Hot Mess Mantra:

I am a new creation-

2 Corinthians 5:17

I cannot sit back and let you keep sitting, too. I cannot let you continue with this messed up identity crisis. I care about you, your life, and your future.

No More Hot Mess

- So when I find myself in a mess, my house in a mess, (including laundry that goes undone for days) my marriage in a mess, (which is an ongoing place of warfare that deserves attention but often gets neglected), my personal spiritual walk and lack of faith in a mess, my physical health in struggles, friendships unattended to, the list could go on and on with my mishaps. Some I create and others just happen. It is easy to see myself as an unworthy mess. What are some things that come to mind that make you feel like a mess right now?

- I look for my belief. My why. I am going through the struggles with you every day, but I still take action. Don't try and put me in a different category than you, because I really am no different when it comes to choices. We all have the same ones. I choose to step up face-to-face with the struggles and see them for what they are, HARD, because life is hard. But I believe that my God will fight harder if I let him. And there is nothing that forms against me that can stand. (Isaiah 54:17; Romans 8:38-39) I want to do the right things, even when it's hard because I know what he has done for me.

- Sister! It is OK for life to be hard. (John 16:33) It is and always will be, but it is NOT OK to not do the right thing. It is not OK to continue believing and living your new middle name is hotmess.
  - Have you made the decision in your mind that a mess is just who you are and have developed a sense of identity in being a mess? Do you take a sense of pride in being a mess?

- I have already mentioned starting simply with Jesus with Scripture reading and writing and then adding gratitude. These two things will literally transform your life because you will be giving yourself a chance to hear from Jesus. And if you are listening, he is going to start telling some pretty crazy cool things. Then if you are ready, he will start talking your hand and showing you how to DO some crazy cool things.

- Beyond the affirmations, Scripture reading and writing and gratitude (bonus loves notes, which by the way, you can do for friends and other family members, your kids, even people on social media, or other moms who need some extra love) Be brave and bold and run with this. You never know how God wants to use you to bless others, and then, of course, bless you in the process with something so simple yet so profound.

- Let's keep this going so you get in the habit of affirming God's truth every day, sister, because this has become the cornerstone of where I am today and the changes that God had been wanting to do in and through me. He wanted to show me that so much of the difficult stuff, the things that we don't want to do, are things that he is wanting to help us with. He knows they are difficult, so he wants to help us, teach us, and do something really amazing in the process that will ultimately help us LIVE out our true identity and purpose.

I am unselfish (Philippians 2:3)

I am LOVED (Jeremiah 31:3)

I am beautiful (Proverbs 31:30)

I am forgiven (1 John 1:7-9)

I am redeemed (1 John 4:4)

I am unique (Romans 12:6)

Chapter 5

I am a precious masterpiece that the Lord God himself hand-crafted with unique qualities and gifts (Isaiah 43:1).

I am a new creation (2 Corinthians 5:17)

Write below the #nomorehotmess affirmation and Scriptures from this chapter and share how this truth makes you feel empowered to live differently:

_____

_____

_____

_____

_____

_____

_____

_____

_____

_____

_____

_____

_____

_____

_____

_____

_____

_____

_____

_____

_____

_____

_____

_____

Chapter 5

Chapter 6
The F- Word

There once was this criminal who had committed a crime. (Because, hey, that's what criminals do. That's their job!) Anyway, he was sent to the king for his punishment. The king told him he had a choice between two punishments: He could be hung by a rope, or take what's behind the big, dark, scary, iron door. The criminal quickly decided on the rope. As the noose was being slipped on him, he turned to the king and asked: "By the way, out of curiosity, what's behind that door?" The king laughed and said: "You know, it's funny, I offer everyone the same choice, and nearly everyone picks the rope." "So," said the criminal, "Tell me. What's behind the door? I mean, obviously, I won't tell anyone," he said, pointing to the noose around his neck. The king paused then answered: "Freedom, but it seems most people are so afraid of the unknown that they immediately take the rope."

~*How to be Happy, Dammit* by Karen Salmansohn

Fear, just like the doubt, shame, feeling overwhelmed, our hotness, y'all, make us believe we ARE the problem. Fear is the reason why we don't think we can change or move forward. It makes us believe that we can't act and often makes us believe that we are actually OK with being miserable.

We would rather have a rope tied around us, choking us, not allowing us to breathe, than to do the harder thing, the scarier thing, the thing that we know we need to do. We choose the rope instead of walking, even though it's walking in fear.

When I found myself crying uncontrollably and experiencing what I felt like was the death of my dream, I felt hopeless. It doesn't happen often, because I make every effort to not be controlled by such ridiculousness, but I was. For a few days, there I was. Satan had taken my mind and warped it to believe that I was a liar. I was a hypocrite. I had believed that I was a speaker and a writer and coach that had love and encouragement to share, and would soon be sharing truth at a ranch that the Lord would graciously provide. YES, these are the things that the Lord had guided me to and had also put on my heart, none of which I had pursued on my own. They were brought to me. They were His plan. But I started to doubt. From struggling with money and lack of support to searching for acceptance and love and affirmation in all the wrong places, I found myself under the influence of the enemy, the one who was trying to do EVERYTHING in his power to stop me dead in my tracks and prevent me from moving forward in any way. I was living as a hotmess.

This is exactly where the enemy likes to point us and how he likes to make us feel.

We see a mess of emotions, a messy house, a messy wife, a messy mom, messy EVERYTHING. And if he can get us to focus on all of our mess, then he has won. Right?

Usually the inadequacies and insecurities will turn into doubt, shame, fear, and well… they take over. The enemy takes over and makes us feel completely insane, but completely sane all at the same time.

The lies he feeds us seem so real and true, don't they?

All I know is that I spent a solid week grieving my dreams. Everything the Lord has shown me, brought me through, and put in my heart, the enemy made me believe it was all made up. I felt embarrassed and ashamed, so I did not tell anyone until I finally told my husband that I was not happy with him or our life anymore. Yep, the enemy worked really hard here because this was the center of my dream, my husband and I working together. So Satan made me believe that leaving him made complete sense and that this was a good starting point.

Satan had literally pointed out EVERY SINGLE thing wrong with my husband: everything he wasn't doing, how much better life would be without him, and how much more peace he could have in his life if I was not in it. I became a victim of LIES and I felt like I could not control it. Maybe Satan is trying to drag you out of your marriage and you are buying it. Maybe he is making you question your very existence. Maybe he is feeding you lies about the dream in your heart being a made-up lie.

Listen to me sister. It is a LIE. The enemy is after you, your heart, your mind, your family, your dream, and he is trying to take the wheel. He wants you to live in fear and walk around with a rope tied to you for the rest of your life. But just like some friends and family did for me, I am here advocating for you! I have already prayed for you as I was writing this book and I will not let you believe these lies any longer.

Looking back, I could see the lies and the seeds that were planted by the enemy many months before. Lies of doubt, of fear. Confusion with things weren't going exactly how I had envisioned or planned. The enemy used all these doubts, fears, and insecurities as ammunition. He knew I was in a weak and vulnerable state. He knew I had forgotten to put on my armor and he was attacking.

This was yet another moment of truth for me, y'all.

Not to get all theological on you, but I want to help you understand something that has been so instrumental in my walk with Jesus and helped me crush my hotmess badge. Since crushing that badge is what you are going to do at the end of this book, I want you to be more prepared.

Confusion Causing Self-Striving, Self-Sabotage, and Emptiness

We were born sinners, and our flesh, our sinful nature, is a hotmess. Truly, we were born this way and our nature is very similar to a crazy monster, and I use the term because I know we have all felt like a monster before by feeling led by something we can't control. An inner struggle, if you will. We don't want to act crazy, but we do. When our house, our lives, and our marriages get messy, we feel messy. And for me, I tend to feel like a hotmess monster, and when I feel like a hotmess monster, then you know what comes next. The crazy comes out like a raging beast and gives birth to monstrous attitudes and behaviors, as well as thoughts and feelings. Yes. Our hotmess ends up dictating how we feel and act, doesn't it?

Not only that, but our hotmess is also the same thing inside of us who makes us believe that we have to perform, we have to do more, our kids have to be in better schools, we have to drive a better car, we need more, the grass is greener, we compare… are you following me?

Our flesh, our hotmess, is just what it says: a mess. This mentality and this way of living is not good and is actually hurtful to our heavenly daddy. Why? Because this way of living will never satisfy. No matter how much you volunteer, how much money you make, how much weight you lose, how much your kids have or how many the experiences they have, if everything you are living for is for stuff, a fleshly earthly feeling of satisfaction, then it means nothing because you will be onto the next best thing, the next quick fix, and NOTHING will seem to satisfy.

Although we may feel OK with the glorified hotmess for a bit, it will keep us from seeking our helper, our maker, our healer, and our heavenly daddy.

You might catch a glimpse of yourself in the mirror and cringe at yourself because you have gained some weight or have been working really hard to lose weight, but it doesn't seem to be making a difference. You start down the hotmess mantra of lies: you are fat, you are disgusting, no wonder your husband doesn't seem to want to touch you, he must not be attracted to you anymore, but who can blame him? Might as well just finish off the Reese's Cups. I mean if you are going to feel this way, you might as well fill your empty soul with the rest of the bag (which I have been known to do MANY times before). Or maybe you think, "OK, well, I am unhappy and disgusted with myself, and apparently there is something majorly wrong with me, and something tells me that the only way you can have peace, happiness, and feel good about yourself is to make your dream body happen" (Which you have on your vision board, btw). And to help you, you need some new workout shoes and clothes. You have decided that if you can work hard enough, be consistent enough, and look that way, then you will be happy. You can win back your husband, be more attractive, feel better, and maybe feel like living your life fully again. If you just lose the weight you can have the life you want.

Our flesh, our hotmess, at times makes us believe that we have it all figured it out. We rationalize our thoughts and behaviors as an attempt to be complete, to satisfy, to feel like we are enough.

Our inner spirit longs for more. We long for belonging and love, so we do many things to fill this void.

In Romans 7:17-22, Paul wants us to understand the difference between living in our flesh and living in the spirit. We know right and wrong, we know the things that harm us and cause grief and pain, but we do them anyways. We act in our sinful, human nature. We look for things of the world to satisfy us. But this is not who we are.

We are in Christ. He is in us. Living in the Spirit allows us to hand things over because Jesus is the chief operator. We don't have to strive or search for fulfillment in the things of this world. We don't have to fall into the arms of the influence of sin. Christ's death on the cross delivered us from the black cloud of sin. We are free in Him!

For if I know the law (right and wrong with my thinking and my actions), but I still can't keep it. If the power of sin within me keeps sabotaging my best intentions, I obviously need help! We know that losing weight will not lead to the love and peace that our souls long for. We know this, yet we continue, hoping that it will do the trick.

Then Paul says, I realize that I don't have what it takes. (verse 18) I can will it (want it), but I can't *do* it. I decide to do good, but I don't *really* do it; I decide not to do bad, but then I do it anyway. (verse 19) My decisions, such as they are, don't result in actions. Something has gone wrong deep within me and gets the better of me every time.

21-23 *It happens so regularly that it's predictable. The moment I decide to do good, sin is there to trip me up. I truly delight in God's commands, but it's pretty obvious that not all of me joins in that delight. Parts of me covertly rebel, and just when I least expect it, they take charge.*

[24] *I've tried everything and nothing helps. I'm at the end of my rope. Is there no one who can do anything for me? Isn't that the real question?* (The Message)

Jesus knew Paul would struggle, He knew we would struggle, and so like all of the other God-inspired and God-breathed words in the Bible, they were meant to bring LIFE and Truth about who God is. So yes, I believe he asked Paul to write Romans as a letter to us, explaining what is happening, why it happens, and to bring us a message of hope.

God wanted us to understand that there is a REAL HOTMESS that lives in you. The crazy, monstrous rage is real. The never-ending feeling that you cannot be disciplined enough or you can't be enough is why it is so easy to cling onto your hotmess. It is easy to feel connected to it, to feel like we should honor it with a t-shirt. We have a fleshy, monstrous hotmess that lives in all of us. But sister, listen, that is part of your old self. When you said "Yes" to Jesus, you said yes to HIS truth. You are enough, you can have victory over all of the things that you leave behind. You can fight this mess and it doesn't have to consume you, it doesn't have to dictate your life. *Your mess is not who you are.*

Jesus made a deadly sacrifice for us so that we do not have to be controlled by this hotmess ever again.

(Romans 7:25) The answer, thank God, is that Jesus Christ can fight our hotmess, and does. He acted to set things right in this life of contradictions where I want to serve God with all my heart and mind, but am pulled by the influence of sin to do something totally different.

This is what I realized:

The devil is alive and well and he is seeking us out making us feel like we are someone we are not. Of course he wanted to create division in my marriage. Marriage is the most sacred covenant and because it's such a powerful bond and means so much to God, the enemy is always looking to break this up. So yes, I became a victim. Just like you become a victim. To your weight, to your debt, to anything that you have soul ties to. The enemy will use this as ammunition against you. Just like the enemy tried to make me believe that my marriage did not matter and neither did my husband, he will do this to you with the things that matter to you most.

What I do know is that Satan is intentional.

Yes, the enemy is working hard to distract, deceive, and destroy. Yes, the enemy will constantly do everything he can to make us doubt the gifts, dreams, abilities, and calling God gives us. But He is not as powerful as we often give him credit for. You better believe that he wanted me to give up or walk away from the dream that God put on my heart. He is on the prowl to do the exact same thing to you, too.

The enemy absolutely wanted me to go back to the hotmess mentality and sit there a while, hoping that I would start to believe that that is who I really am. And the degree at which he is trying to make this happen is absolutely scary. The enemy is very intentional and is out to steal and destroy. He will take extreme measures, sister, especially when it comes to things that will further the kingdom of God like your marriage, your family, your health, your God-given gifts. You have opportunities to use them to expand and influence the world for the Lord. So if you are doing that, if you are making a difference, making an impact, then you better believe the enemy will pay lots of visits.

Marriage is hard because the enemy seeks to destroy it. Living a healthy lifestyle is so hard because good health is required for certain assignments that the enemy doesn't want you to do, and your entire families legacy can be changed by YOU starting this lifestyle. Having a healthy relationship with money and owing no one is so hard, because the enemy doesn't want us to have extra money to use for good, and because he wants to use money as a wedge to keep strife in our marriages. Raising kids is so hard because these precious children are the future generation and you better believe the enemy wants us to crush their spirits and cause friction so that the future generation is impacted.

Do you hear me?

Every area of our life matters, EVERY AREA. And the enemy wants us to believe that there are varying degrees of importance. He wants us to place things in categories and wants us to believe that it is OK not to pay certain areas any attention. WHY? Because ultimately our own future and our families future are impacted by this.

But here's the truth! The enemy has no power over Jesus. Absolutely none!

We give him way more credit than he deserves, sister.

I cannot stress to you enough the battles I fought to finish this book. Ms. Hotmess express showed up so many times in various ways. The enemy works overtime to distract and deceive us, sister, and it is to 100% destroy, to make us show up in a constant state of disappointment, of discontent, of shamefulness, anxiousness, of pure doubt in ourselves, and of our God. To cause us to never do what God has called us to do. And this, my dear friend, is what happens when we wear our hotmess badge with honor. We are willingly letting our mess dictate our lives and by saying "yes" to the enemy's lies and turning our back to freedom we have in Christ.

The Lord was asking me to write this book. He was asking me to TRUST him, to rest in Him. (Psalm 46:10) He never told me to stop loving, encouraging, and serving others, he just said do the things that matter NOW and TRUST ME with the rest, with your future, with my promises to you! (Deuteronomy 31:8) I am a God who does what I say I will do, now TRUST ME. (Joshua 23:14)

It took the enemy attacking every area of my life for me to recognize my disobedience, what I was seeing as my lack of discipline. I am a disciplined person, I would say. But, I had covered up my belief with lies. My lack of trust and faith was me saying "no" to God.

When I really started thinking about this book and what God was trying to teach me, I was thinking it was about self-discipline, to share my struggles, and to teach people about how to be more disciplined. But what God wanted to show me is that self-discipline is rooted in belief. If you believe in something, you have a reason to take action.

You have desire rooted in something more than self. It is not something that we are born with, it is not something we just have because we decide to have it one day. We develop a deep sense of hope, of purpose, of trust, belief and then we act based on our belief when we recognize Jesus as Lord.

When you understand God, who He is, His promises, how much He unconditionally loves you, and sacrificially died to save your wrenched sinful soul, you will desire a different life. You want to behave differently. You begin to act out of His promises, out of what He said he had already done, not what we can do out of obligation or to make ourselves feel better. We have a desire to allow the Lord to work in us, to complete us, and be all for us. And remembering that just because God is in it, or we are called to do it, that it will not automatically be easy.

So many people come to the conclusion that if life becomes hard, if things seem impossible, that this is permission from God to quit. Isn't that the tendency of most of us? Well, it is taking longer for me to lose weight that it is supposed to, so it's never going to happen, so I quit. Well, my husband will not clue in, he will not do his part, and I cannot live neglected, I deserve better, so I quit. I think it is possible to live out my dream, to actually impact lives doing something I love, but I am so overwhelmed. I actually don't think I am capable to actually do it, so I quit or force myself to quit thinking about it. I have been in the trenches for months, years, going after this dream, serving others, doing all that I know to do, and I can't catch a break, I don't feel like what I am doing matters. So I think I need to just quit.

What else have you thought?

What have you quit?

Listen, quitting CANNOT BE AN OPTION.

Ms. Hotmess is a quitter because she chooses to be miserable. She wants you to believe you can never find the inner peace you desire. She wants you to believe that you are not capable and that God has forgotten about you. She wants you to be confused and yes, she wants you to quit and keep quitting. Matter of fact, she wants you to become so familiar with quitting that you don't even think twice about quitting. Especially when it comes to yourself, because this brings you back to where you started, over and over and over. Quitting doesn't allow you to trust God. Quitting doesn't allow you to believe in yourself or believe in God. When you don't believe and instead listen to Ms. Hotmess, you are basically agreeing to listen to lies from Satan.

That's what this is really all about!

Discipline is a crazy word that everyone avoids and wants to say they don't have, but sister, discipline is actually BELIEF. Belief in Jesus and belief that he will do in you what he said he will do.

Declare Your Truth Your New BELIEF

I know getting up early to talk to Jesus and to read and receive His truth as your personal truth matters. I believe that Jesus matters and time with Him matters so much. So, I will do it. Not out of obligation, but out of the inner desire to know Him more, to feel connected and close, and to be excited about what he might tell me, what he might show me. I believe that an intimate relationship with Jesus is possible and needed and that I am worthy of this type of relationship with the Lord. I BELIEVE.

I know that living a healthy lifestyle is good for my mind, heart, and soul. It is not about numbers on the scale or how I look, but about what health provides for me. It not only benefits my physical body, but healthy living is required for me to live the life God has called me to. I BELIEVE that it matters. I believe that God will help me do it, so I will show up. I deserve good health. I am worthy of good health. I BELIEVE it is possible and that I am worthy of it. I BELIEVE.

I know that making intentional effort to love, support, and grow in my marriage matters. I know that I don't always personally benefit from the efforts I put out, but I know that I deserve an intimate and thriving marriage. I believe that it is possible and that I am worthy of it. I BELIEVE.

I know that developing a healthy relationship with money is important. I know that money must be made to live and is needed for many things. I believe that money matters and that money is not bad. I believe that owing people money is a type of bondage that often keeps me from peace. I believe that it is possible to live without debt and that it is important. I believe that I deserve money. I believe that living a debt-free life is possible and that I am worthy of living this type of life. I BELIEVE.

I know that clinging to the God-inspired ideas, dreams, visions, and possibilities that the Lord put on my heart is so important and matters so much. The Lord uses people like me to reach the lost and to encourage the redeemed. I believe that God gave me unique abilities to be used and gives me ways to use them. I believe that I matter so much to God. I know that if I quit on me and the things God put on my heart, then I am turning my back on God and what he said he would do. I believe that I deserve to be used. I deserve to dream big dreams and believe that it is possible to live them out. I believe that I am worthy of living a God-inspired life. I BELIEVE.

I knew that God called me to write this book, but I wasn't making myself available. I was allowing my hotmess to win. Ultimately, my mess left the door to my heart and mind wide open, and the enemy ran right in and took over. I believe with my whole heart that so much of my attack was because I started living as a hotmess. I believe that I could figure out everything on my own and when I couldn't, when things weren't going as planned or as easy as I thought they should be, I decided that I wasn't capable. I decided that if it was this hard, then maybe I shouldn't be doing this.

Instead of taking off my hotmess badge, looking up, making myself available, letting go of my selfish desires, my insecurities, and letting God show me what to write, I was trying to control everything and flaunting the hotmess coffee mug, all while making more of a mess.

I did not trust. I did not believe.

God said he wanted to write a book with me. He wanted to give me the words and ideas. He wanted to provide a way to tell His story through my story, but I did not have faith that God would do what He promised He would do. So hotmess became my mantra, my safe place, and my excuses. I began to receive it as who I was and how I was going to live and I had even told myself that I needed to stay this way so that people could relate to me. If I was a hotmess like everyone else, then people might follow me, might like me more. WHAT!?

And maybe you are thinking, ok, well, I am not planning on writing a book, Cheneil. I am not in any way, shape, or form going to help others like you do, or speak or whatever else your big crazy heart is going to do. I am just a small-town girl who is pretty "ok" with just living my small life.

What about your health, your marriage or other relationship, your finances?

What about the dream on your heart, sister? The dream that you can't get out of your head, but you keep telling yourself that it is not possible. The dream that you have been telling yourself can't ever come true. The dream to be debt-free so you can take vacations or give to anyone in need without even thinking twice, to have a thriving and connected marriage, to be pain-free or truly feel good from the inside out and able to run around with your kids because you are in the best shape of your life. The dream to boldly live out your passion and fearlessly do what the Lord is asking you to do without fear or doubt.

The dream to live in freedom.

Maybe this sounds or seems ridiculous or far-fetched, or maybe you don't even think you deserve some of these things. Guess what, I certainly didn't.

For so many years I had found myself doing more, trying to be more, and striving to feel better about myself and prove that I was worthy. I believed that I needed to earn God's favor more than I believed in Him and what he can do through me. My focus was all wrong. I had decided that since life often became hard and things don't usually go as planned, when I found myself up against something that was trying to make me believe I was less than and I would never measure up, I thought that maybe this was true. Maybe I am not worthy. Maybe I will never be enough. Maybe I cannot do or have the things I wanted.

When I said "Yes" to Jesus, the Holy Spirit entered in and the Spirit is POWER. This spirit produces LIFE. Power and life is everything that a career didn't give me, everything that more money didn't give me, everything that my husband can't give me, everything that reassurance or permission can't give me.

Christ in me is life. (2 Corinthians 13:5) THIS is who I am. I am LIFE. And the way I live this out is through the spirit. And yes, the spirit wants to help you take action. Not action related to law or flesh, but action from a place of redemption. A place of awe, of reverence, wanting others to see the difference in you so that you can then point them back to Jesus. When I told you that you would need to be willing to take action in the beginning of this book, I meant it. He wants us to take action.

Not taking out of a place of obligation, but more so a place of belief and responsibility. Knowing that God loves us so much that he entrusted us with a purpose that only He can fulfill in us. When we know this, we can receive our gifts as gifts, as God giving us special things so that we can partner with him in the miraculous work he is going to do here on earth. He wants others to experience Him and His love. Since he is not walking the earth anymore, he is inviting us to be Jesus to others.

In order to be Jesus to those around us, we need to see our gifts for what they are: as opportunities from the Lord to share Him. We have to be willing to use our talents, which first requires that we become aware of them so that we can then understand and trust and believe in what God can and wants to do through us.

And I do not know many people who are living a life of complete trust and obedience.

Our flesh, or hotmess, will always be present, causing us to fight this inner battle. (2 Corinthians 10:3-5) But regardless, HE has already won. (John 16:33) The minute we start feeling ourselves shifting to the hotmess, we can always remember that this is NOT who we are. The lies, the frustrations, the shame, the guilt, our past, even our spouses, friends and family, our battle is not against these things. Our battle is against the enemy. But sister, our battle has already been won!

Hallelujah, we are victorious.

There is no such thing as a perfectly obedient Christian Life, but there is such thing as living a life of peace and freedom, a life lived out from a place of belief in Christ. Not from our own selfish ambition, but purely out of humility because he first loved us.

Romans 8:11-14 says that the very alive and present God who raised Jesus from the dead lives in us, y'all. The spirit is beckoning and is ready to take you places. He is waiting on you to stop giving authority to your hotmess so that God can fulfill His promises, so that He can take you places.

It's time to say NO to the hotmess self that is holding you back! Getting a little more technical, the truth is that when you said "yes" to Jesus, your hotmess died. It was crucified on the cross with Jesus. YES! It is as though it went to the grave. This is your truth.

My dear sister, You are NOT a hotmess! You are a precious, redeemed daughter of the most high KING. The spirit of God lives in you and you have LIFE. The life we long for, it is in you.

You already have it. 2 Peter 1:3-4

Chapter 6

Chapter 7

I Get It from My Momma

Believers in humble circumstances ought to take pride in their high position. [10] *But the rich should take pride in their humiliation—since they will pass away like a wild flower.* [11] *For the sun rises with scorching heat and withers the plant; its blossom falls and its beauty is destroyed. In the same way, the rich will fade away even while they go about their business.*

James 1:9-11

Let's talk about a few things that have left an imprint on my life, because I am sure this will scuff up some funny memories for you, too. We had a wood-grained station wagon in which I was taken to lots of sports and school in, where I was, YES, let out from the back of that clunker in junior high and some of high school. EMBARASSING! But even funnier, later I realized that my mom chose the wagon because she didn't want to be a minivan mom. But don't worry, we ended up with a huge brown minivan anyways.

Then my first car was a used, reddish-that-ended-up-kind-of-orangish, stick shift Plymouth laser that I learned to drive on an access road incline in Dallas while my dad was yelling at me and my mom was following me with my brothers. Oh, Lord. Then after that scare, I had to keep a wrench within reach because the nobs on my lever to roll down the windows fell off soon after we got it, and the air conditioning didn't work well, so if I wanted to breathe in the dead heat of a Texas summer, I had to use a wrench to roll down the windows and teach my friends how to do it when they rode with me. But I learned to laugh about it and so did they. Then there was ole blue. It was a navy-blue Honda accord with deep black tinted windows, gold chains around the license plate, and YES, white powder was found in the trunk the day we brought it home. And yes, people followed me and looked at me a bit weird when I was in certain parts of the "drug dealer" part of town. I am pretty sure I was driving a cartel repo. Lord help me. Oh, and how can I forget. You know that wrench that was used for the windows in my laser? Well, I had no idea that I would need to keep it. This car required "electric friction" to start the car. Yep, I had to use the wrench and scrape the starter for the stinkin' car to start, y'all. Please don't even try to imagine this because it was absolutely insane, annoying, and we didn't want the dealer that we traded it for my first brand new car to find out that the next time they would try to start it, they would need a wrench. I will never forget the prayers that were prayed by my husband on the way to the dealership that day, "Lord this is a good car and it has a great starter. I know you work miracles so make this car have a good starter."

Oh, and I can't forget my brothers silver Dodge aspen that was actually my grandfathers, so yep, it was old. It needed at running start. We literally had to push it out of the driveway and then down a bit of the road to somehow "help it" start. I ain't making this stuff up.

These cars y'all.

I am sure you have many stories of the array of cars and all of their unique personalities that left a lasting impression and little scars to your ego. Or maybe that was just me.

I have two very hardworking, wonderful parents who did the best they knew how. I lived life like I think a lot of us do, mostly out of survival. It's so hard not to. I experienced mistakes, hurt, pain, confusion, just like many of you did. And I could sit here and tell you lots of stories from my perspective and how they affected me, words that were said that I can't ever seem to get out of my head, lack of words that I wish were said, and physical pain that I won't forget. The rat race we ran. But I think we all have those stories. We all have deep emotions connected to how we were raised and what went on in our homes. You know what yours are and that's the perspective I want you to look back on. I don't want to bring up pain, but I want you to understand that just like the hotmess life we often live now and the enemy wants so desperately for us to stay in, our past is an even bigger beast that can only complicate things so much more if we let it.

I understand that there is a lot of pain that people experience from the past. Trust me. I know! I do not want to just hop over this, but I also want to share how it can affect us.

Chapter 7

I understand that not everyone reading this book is a wired like me, ready to jump out of bed each day, a go-getter, ready to discover ways to concur any and all messes that comes your way, all in your own power and strength, of course. There are some of you who look at your mess and literally go into an anxiety attack or just turn and walk away, emotionally blocking it out altogether. You know that there is a mess, but you refuse to get physically and emotionally engaged because, well, you don't have time for that.

And some of you are saying, Cheneil, hello, I must really be messed up because I am both. Sometimes I am a cheerleader jacked up on pre workout or double shot expresso seasonal flavored coffee (hello Pumpkin Spice) leaping for the sky and believing I can personally change my own water into wine if I just try hard enough. And when it comes to certain things that really matter, like my health, marriage, and pursuing that dream in my heart, well, I have continued to see myself as a hotmess. I hope and pray things get better, but usually just walk away.

So YES... you had me at #hotmess Cheneil. That is basically who I am.

So much of my own life has been wrapped up in, "What have I done wrong?" or "What am I not doing right?" I have often thought about what I did wrong in my past or what I could have done differently with things that I had zero control over. Which, of course, leaves me smack in the middle of the mess again and again if I am not careful. I can usually look back or look around, and my entire world often revolved around ME and my mess instead of the Miracle Worker.

The hotmess life is selfish. Sorry, but it is. Hey, I lived in it too, so I can say that. Living like a hotmess is about us. How we feel and giving ourselves the permission to live how we want. The outcome ends up gratifying disobedience, willingly allowing ourselves to live a messy life, on our own terms, and then stamping our t-shirts and mugs like #hotmess is a badge of honor. And if you haven't figured it out, this is how the world and the enemy wants us to live. The enemy screams, "Add one more thing to your plate. It will make you feel enough. Give yourself a little more grace, you don't really need to improve anyway. Buy more things because you deserve them, do more and you will be happier."

Life is messy and full of plenty natural messes. But as long as we allow ourselves to use hotmess as the chain that keep us from allowing Christ to show us what he wants and allowing him to work in us, we will stay in the vicious cycle of wrinkled laundry that we keep starting and starting but not actually doing, hanging up, or even OHHHHHH can't believe I am even saying this… ironing. Cause I don't really do that, but yes! I fully believe that we are all a mess, just like the load of laundry. And if the same load has been sitting there for a week, then you certainly start feeling like a complete ridiculous mess, don't you? The problem is, this is NOT our identity. We've got mess, but a HOTMESS is not "WHO" Christ says we are.

Sister, in Him and through Him we are made righteous. (Romans 5:1) You are loved! (1 John 3:1) You are held! (Psalm 139:10) You are clean! (John 15:2-4; Hebrews 10:17) You are more than a conqueror! (Romans 8:37) You are ENOUGH!

No More Hot Mess Mantra:

You are loved! You are held! You are
clean! You are more than a conqueror!
You are ENOUGH!

Can I get an Amen?

But why is it so hard to receive this truth? Why is it so hard to stop allowing our minds to go down the messy trap of lies? Why do we use our kids, work, our parents and the way we were raised, the things of our past, to literally dictate how we live life today?

Why do we do what Paul described earlier? We know what not to do, but we do it anyways. We know what to do, yet we don't do it. So of course we feel like crazy mommas. I believe that together, if you are willing to look up and walk where God wants to take you, He will show you.

And I want you to know that if you are feeling like you don't have the mental energy, the willpower, the time to unravel this truth, please know that the enemy is already working and trying to keep you tied to the hotmess job title. Just like the diet coke habit, or the nicotine habit, and the sugar addictions, we know what we shouldn't do, but we do it anyways and spend most of our days justifying it. The enemy wants nothing more than to drag you along with him as he tries to deceive you every chance he can get. His ultimate goal is for you to never experience freedom in Jesus and therefore never live out His purpose for you and your life that God has already planned out.

It's planned and waiting, sister. Think about that. The good life, the bright pink, red velvet cupcake life, is waiting for you, and the Lord is constantly trying to guide you there. I can't help but think of the game Candyland and the gingerbread men on their way to the candy castle. And think about us on our way to heaven. Do you remember the square of "shame" that they had to stop on since they were eating so much sugar? What about the square of genetics that seems to be the reason why you stay stuck in the mess? Or the square of pain from a situation and it won't let them keep moving forward? The square of fear and doubt?

You are right, these squares do not exist. But stick with me. In the real game, once the game starts, there is NOTHING separating the gingerbread men from getting to the castle. There are a few stops and skips, but they had a destination and everyone ended up in the castle. But let's think hypothetically. What if there were actually squares that the gingerbread landed on that would make them stay stuck and never reach the castle? Once this happens, there is no hope, you quit playing the game. You quit moving forward.

Think about us. When we land on the fear and doubt in our own life, we don't move. It's crippling and often paralyzing.

Now I know what you are probably thinking. "Cheneil. I mean, Candyland and the candy castle. You already talked about the old cars and now this? First of all, those who struggle with sugar addiction, you have just caused us to sin. I am now thinking about any and every sugary anything I could get my hands on, asap. Shame on you. And second, this is ridiculous and crazy."

But this got me to really thinking about our past: the good, the bad, the ugly. And about redemption.

What if we chose a different path? What if we quit allowing stuff like genetics, our parents, our pain, our shortcomings, and our fears completely become the reason why we make negative, drowning, cyclic choices? What if we quit letting this stuff, the stuff that is keeping us in bondage, dictate how we live life?

You can choose hotmess because it makes the most sense, and most of the time it is the easiest thing. But sister, you don't have to.

This is why, in Jesus, there is no such thing as generational curses. Not that you are not affected by things of the past or from previous generations, but God can use you to change the legacy of your family. You receive a NEW nature that matches that of Jesus. Out of God we are born as a new creation, (2 Corinthians 5:17) a new birth making us 100% in Christ, no longer living on our own, the Holy Spirit now lives in us and through us.

When you said YES to Jesus, the old way of living died. It doesn't mean that we won't struggle, won't have pain or fear, but it means that we don't have to stay in the messy struggle. James 1:2-4;   2 Corinthians 1:3-6

I grew up in a home with two working parents and three kids involved in lots of activities. There was so much going and going and our two wonderful parents who worked very hard and still work very hard. I still watch my dad give everything he has to his business. At an early age, I learned about integrity, character, and discipline, and what working hard and taking care of things looked like. These values are now very important to me and I tend to focus on them without even thinking about it. I often feel that I am "wired" that way. I watched my dad and innately felt drawn to leadership, or dictatorship, as my husband and kids might say. My mom was the doer. She did everything, and I mean everything. We had a four-course meal most nights a week while she was working a full-time job. Laundry was done and folded every night. She always got us where we needed to go and remembered everything, doing her best to keep peace.

I think about life and how it was done in my house when I was growing up with the cars, all the crazy cars. I think at the time, as a kid, it was usually about getting what we think we want and need, but not fully understanding all that is going on or how it would impact us later. It is easy for me to look back and do A LOT of blaming. But if I stay there, in the frustration, hurt, pain, and confusion, I can't truly LIVE.

I am not saying that there is no validation to your pain, to your frustration, to whatever emotion you are feeling and have felt. But what I am saying is that when you said "Yes" to Jesus, the way you can move forward in life changed. You now have the Holy Spirit living in YOU! You don't have to compete with your past. You have a new name; your slate is now clean. (Revelation 2:17) This means you don't have to have the same relationship with money, or your spouse, or careers, or your kids that you had before Christ. NOPE. You do not have to repeat or blame or use this as a reason why YOU CAN'T!

And because I love you, I am letting you know that you cannot do this anymore.

You should no longer use these things against yourself. Do not use them as reasons why you will not have a great marriage, have a peaceful relationship with money, allow the Lord to use you, get healthy for your family and stay healthy, and use your gifts fully with no strings attached. Your old self is gone, and your new self is here with everything you need to be free.

No more hot mess.

Have you found yourself either feeling like you are the gingerbread man who keeps getting stopped or stuck in the square of lies?

Have you taken a step back and evaluated if you are using your past, your genetics, and generational issues as reasons why you are living a certain way?

Who have we made this life about?

What have you made this beautiful life about?

We have talked about living the hotmess life, but when you bring your past into the mix, oh sister, we all know what happens. It's like walking through life after having a baby, yet it never ends. You stay drained but are forced to be alert. You have someone to feed every two hours, but you've run out of milk with no way to go to the store. You have a house to clean, but you can't even hold your head up. You have a file cabinet that is required to stay open in your head, but you still can't remember everything. You have a husband who also needs attention, but you hate your body and can't stand to let him see it, so you body-shame instead. Y'all, the after-baby business is so hard. So, so hard. I feel like we take ourselves back to that horrible place when we allow ourselves to live in the hotmess life and constantly bring up the past.

You are not obligated, bound to, are supposed to stay in, or cursed by your past.

Maybe you find yourself using your past as your reason why you can't, won't, shouldn't, haven't. Maybe you have viewed your life from the lens of what your mom did or didn't do, what your dad did or didn't do.

Counseling has greatly helped me. I had no idea that some of the memories tied to my past were impacting so much of my current life. We were married eleven years when I told my husband that I wanted to leave and would unless he was willing to go to counseling. It took us eleven years to humbly recognize that the Lord wanted better for us and that we were both allowing so many strongholds, mostly selfishness, to win. We were allowing the enemy to win. But this experience changed our lives, it completely changed everything. It pointed us to Jesus, which is where the focus should have been all along. This experience showed us what redemption and love really was. Now, because we went to counseling does not mean we have been exempt from the enemy and his intentional work. As a matter of fact, I feel that because of our intentional efforts to become a stronger, more Christ-centered couple, the enemy attacks more. We are still learning to navigate marriage and it is hard, but it is also so beautiful to see Jesus working in us. We believed that our marriage mattered. We BELIEVED that our individual walks with Jesus mattered. We believed, so we did. We acted because we believed.

So, if you have not been to counseling, or have had a counselor for check-ups, please, please, please, do yourself a favor and get one.

And honestly, whether you are waiting for counseling or not, start saying "YES" to you. Work on you. Stop allowing your energy to be placed on what your husband isn't doing, what your parents didn't do. Quit focusing on the other people and things that are easy "blame." Start focusing on you and what you can change. Daily affirm God's truth, even when you don't quite believe it. Write your Scripture and gratitude even when you feel like you can't find something to be grateful for. Be bold and ask for what you need in prayer. (Matthew 6:8)

Why do we wait?

There were piles and piles for weeks. I looked at my couch and even my husband didn't want to touch it. What I have decided is that the laundry actually becomes a beast of its own. It just sits there glaring at us to fold it, but we don't. And before we know it, the laundry starts making us believe that we are lazy and worthless because we haven't tended to it. Oh, and your husband, he's worthless too because he hasn't helped with it. Oh, the laundry. As much as I loathe saying this, the laundry shouldn't wait.

Why? Just like writing that book you've always wanted to write shouldn't wait, going back to school to pursue a passion shouldn't wait, starting your NO sugar lifestyle or exercise routine shouldn't wait, getting healthy for your family can't wait, starting the business that will allow you to be the mom you desire to be can't wait, going to marriage counseling can't wait, having that discussion can't wait! THE THINGS THAT MATTER sister, they CAN'T WAIT.

Like the laundry that starts out as being just laundry, that THING turns into a beast. The reason you don't do laundry is the reason that you don't do a lot of things, and the beast of lies, deception, disappointment, they don't stop. They are like a dark cloud that hovers and won't go away.

So why do we convince ourselves that these things don't "really" matter? Or why does crap have to hit the fan, a full-blown anxiety attack, a marital dispute leading us to believing lies on the verge of throwing things out on the lawn, a self-sabotage session that lasts for days because we feel like we aren't enough, why does it take the extreme of stuff to happen before we feel the need to make a change? Why does it take neglecting yourself and family and feeling like you need to commit yourself into a mental hospital before we feel the need to make a change? I have been in this place, too.

So why? Why does it take these extremes, these times when things keep piling up and then spew into a mess, like the slime that your kids have left all over the house? Why do we have to get to a place of feeling like and living like a total mess to make us realize that we aren't "showing up for ourselves" or that we are not "living up to our full potential"?

Why do we get to this point, or wait for something tragic to happen before we make efforts to walk towards change, walk towards the things that matter?

If I told you I had not experienced EVERY single one of those things and more, I would not be sharing my truth. And what I promise is that HERE, within these pages, you have gotten the truth, my whole heart, my journey, and my story; some of my biggest struggles and issues are here. But here is how I am moving forward passionately and diligently as I am walking in full dependence on Him, as I am walking in BELIEF.

Sister, I am going through this struggle with you, but I am confidently winning! I BELIEVE. That is why you are reading this book. I have learned so much about myself, about life, what's important, and the best part, about Jesus and His love, grace, mercy, and availability to you and me.

I want you to know that I cannot be your sister that gives you a good dose of, "Momma it's ok, let it go, maybe you shouldn't." I'm not going to be the friend who says, "Girl, just give yourself some more grace so that you can continue praying, dreaming, and hoping for a life without issues, problems, and struggles while sitting on your couch eating your body weight in Reece's cups and watching mind-numbing Netflix to help distract your negative reel that you can't stop. Or just drink wine till you pass out so that you can do your hotmess all over again the next day." I say this because, YEP, this is exactly what I have done to make myself feel better, too. I have given myself a lot of excuses why I can't start or finish, a lot of excuses why I went on months of binge eating, why I couldn't finish this book, why I am not successful. I have allowed myself to choose the hotmess instead of truth way too many times, and between people close to me telling me these lies and me telling myself these lies, I had to choose what to believe. I have been down this road, and this IS NOT the truth.

But I have had to make decisions just like you have had to make. I could continue to listen to lies that I am not strong enough to say no to the dessert. That I cannot get up and workout because I didn't get enough sleep, or the kids woke me up. That I cannot write this book because I don't have the right words. That I can't be happy in my marriage because he won't put out the "right" effort. That I will never be a good mom or have a good quality of life because I want to use my gifts and be a mom, too. I have had to make decisions based on what I believed. And let me tell you, when I am living like a mess, allowing junk and lies to run my life, allowing the enemy to win, I cannot make good decisions. I don't make good decisions. And there are always consequences. Not as a punishment from God, oh, sister, don't pull that flag. It is a consequence of our own behaviors. No, you can't lose the weight if you allow anything to go in your mouth every weekend. So no, you are not giving it all you've got. God did not make this happen, you did.

Even I have to step back and see what's really going on. And usually, it's the mess. It's winning.

But what I have learned is that when I have a deep-rooted belief, it helps me show up. It goes beyond how I feel. When I rise up in full belief, I move forward knowing something good is going to happen. Something supernatural happens in your mind and soul that no one can take away when we are brave enough to move, to take action in faith.

You know what I'm talking about. If you have prayed a prayer in expectation and willingly took those steps of trust, you know what I am talking about. If you haven't, I am sure that your time is coming. Because a seed has been planted and is growing in your belief right now, so soon a flower is going to spring up. Romans 8:28-29

With all the mistakes that I have made, the guilt that I have carried, and the lies that I have lived with and told myself, I know that there are reasons why we choose to show up and reasons why we don't. Some are good, and honestly sister, some just aren't good enough reasons. It is OK for life to be hard and to want it to be easier. It is OK to be OVER the struggle and beg for a breakthrough. But it is simply not OK to not show up.

I am sure that you can think of some people in your personal life that have directly impacted the way you live life today. People who, despite tremendous opposition, didn't quit. Some of my healthcare friends may know Dr. Elizabeth Blackwell. She was a woman who experienced significant adversity when she was attempting to be the first female to get into medical school. Back then, a woman should not do such a thing. She was not smart enough, not qualified, and had to go through so many trials against men on this pursuit of equality. But she persisted and believed in herself, her worth, her purpose, and she was the first woman to receive a medical degree. Think about the door that she opened, allowing so many women to use their gifts. And think about all the brilliant, gifted women who should have also been in line with her to complete their degree and serve people but allowed fear to win.

Good 'ole Thomas Edison not only struggled with dyslexia and was told as a young child he would never be successful in life, was struck against countless setbacks and obstacles while creating his brilliant idea. If he would have allowed himself to quit, sister we literally would not have the lightbulb. I mean, sure, someone else might have come along later, but this man BELIEVED. He would not let it go. So, think of Thomas next time you have an idea or you are in the trenches with your dream. You cannot quit. We need you.

Stephen King's first book, *Carrie*, was literally denied by publishers 30 times. The Lord brought me a publisher. I didn't even have to go out and convince anyone to allow me to share my heart and mind, but 30 people turned this man away. We have ALL heard of Stephen King. Think if he would have given up. I am not saying we are necessarily positively impacted by a horror film, but I am saying we can definitely learn something from someone who BELIEVES in themselves, their purpose, and dreams. His life changed in many ways because he stayed the course and kept going.

And Oprah. She was molested as a child, sustained many other adversities in her childhood including losing her own child at the age of 14, but y'all, she is known as one of the most influential women by using her adversity to help others overcome theirs. If she did not listen to the little voice (I believe the Holy Spirit) and run with conviction towards her calling, she would not be who she is today. I like to think that someone like Oprah is someone who has opened the door for some who may have never heard of Jesus to be willing to think about Jesus. Oprah believed in herself, her worth, and a greater purpose.

I have told myself to quit, to just give up, and then…

I remember conversations with myself on many occasions. After failing my Nurse Exam (NCLEX), I had told myself that I should quit trying and should just enlist in the military so they could pay back my school. I had made plans to do so if I didn't pass my Nursing Exam the second time. I was ready to quit.

During nurse practitioner school, because, yes, I wanted to torture myself, (well, prove to myself I could do it), I encountered many obstacles. I had told myself to just quit after making my second C since I had to make a B. I even took a step away from school to convince myself not to quit. Then I told myself I shouldn't have kids since I chose a demanding career. I wouldn't be present because of my crazy work hours. I believed so many lies during many parts of my life. But you know what else I did? I believed in me. Something deep down told me that, YES, I CAN. Quitting was not an option. I had to keep going because I believed I had come that far. I had to keep going because I knew it mattered.

And because I love you, I am not going to tell you that it is OK for you to quit or that you don't have to keep going or that you don't need to do anything to change your circumstances. I could have said many, many times that the timing wasn't right. Since things were so difficult, it must not be the right thing. I could have listened to the inner voice saying, "You are not smart enough," because if you remember, that was exactly what the enemy had already told me before I even got into nursing school. I had already believed a lie that I was not smart enough. I could have believed that I would not be a good mother, so I wouldn't have kids. I could have lived in this fear.

The reality is, SISTER, YOUR LIFE CAN'T WAIT. Just because we meet opposition, just because things are hard, and just because the right thing seems like quitting, it is not. The things God put on your heart, the things you feel in your soul that need to change, the things you can't quit thinking about, the things that cause you the most stress and anxiety, YES those things, they cannot wait.

There are reasons they are bothering you! There is a reason that you are reading this, and quite frankly, the good Lord has big freakin' plans for you and He can't use you when you dig your heels in, when you hide from him, and when you turn your back on him. *And he certainly can't help you if you keep choosing your mess instead of Him.* I have lived too much of my life in a negative head space, in fear, and insecurities. What I know is that someone helped me to continue fighting, to continue showing up. I have felt the hand of the Lord in so much and he continues to pull me out of the darkness and the mess when I choose to let it take over!

Although it may seem that certain people just have it better and seem to have it all together, especially when you start comparing your life to theirs, I wholeheartedly believe that there really isn't much different with you and so many others. So much comes down to simply a choice in what we believe. For those of you who feel you are different, you are probably right. As Christians, you are living differently because of how you think and what you believe about yourself and about God. We have developed a different belief system. We believe in the power of the one who lives in us more than we believe in our fear, our insecurities, our doubts, our past, our circumstances. (1 John 4:4) We all struggle. We all have things going on in our head and life. We all have mess, y'all.

Just because I am writing this does not mean my marriage doesn't struggle, because let me reassure you that the enemy is fighting hard every day to cause division, or that I don't have episodes of anxiety doubting my very existence, that I don't get trapped in the negative reel of thinking, that I don't yell at my kids, or that I don't make mistakes. I do! Oh, sister I do.

But, I care deeply about YOU, about US, and the future generation. I care about what you believe about Jesus, his love for you, and what you believe about yourself. I care deeply about the responsibility that we have and the opportunity that we have been given to be the LIGHT in this incredibly dark and miserable world. (Matthew 5:14) Our responsibility is to be true to who we are and fully recognize that we are fully equipped to do all that God has called of us, as a wife and a mother, in our skills and gifts. Using our gifts and being true to ourselves does not require perfection. Ephesians 2:10

You are not required to be Oprah, or an inventor, or a doctor to write books. Being loved by God has no requirements. Being helped by God has no requirements. Being used by God requires a belief in Him, a belief in what he promised to do, and a willingness to take imperfect action.

No More Hot Mess Mantra:

I can and I will take imperfect action!

So, I refuse to sit back and let you believe that you are just another number or another hotmess in the world.

Every single piece of your life matters. It matters so much that the God of the universe spoke your name into existence and then handcrafted your every fiber into this unbelievably beautiful masterpiece. (Psalm 139:13) And He didn't create and leave you alone. He not only gave you some unique things he needs you to do while on this earth, but those things he has given you to do, they are so important that only you can do them like YOU can do them. Be the wife to your husband and be the mom to your kids that only YOU can be. God has this beautiful life all planned, sister, as a promised gift to us. His plan is to save, to redeem, to prosper, to abundantly bless, and then carry us into eternity with him.

So, if we KNOW these truths, that what the God of the universe promises us is true, why do we turn and walk away when He is asking us to do something? Why do we think less of ourselves when we know He is calling us to something greater? Why do we blatantly say, "NO" when we KNOW he is HERE for us, waiting for us to walk with Him, and waiting for us to receive something amazing?

Maybe it's because it is hard. Maybe it's because we just don't want to. Maybe because it seems impossible. Maybe because it seems like more than we can handle.

Guess what, sister? That exact thing that God calls us to is ALWAYS more than we can handle. It is going to be difficult, uncomfortable, and hard, and because it is hard, YOU NEED JESUS.

He is giving you the chance to ask for help, walk with Him, and trust Him. He is standing behind these walls of rejection and all the lies you hear from Satan that you can't, shouldn't, and won't ever. He is standing behind them with His arms open wide waiting to embrace You and enfold you in the security of His truth. He is standing behind them, sister. (Psalm 139:5)

Picture a girl's trip. Your athletic, adventurous friend convinced everyone to go look at a world traveler's best waterfall. It is so stinkin' humid and a hot, hot Texas heat kind of day. You have been hiking through these communities and in caves and up a few treacherous mountains to get to this waterfall. You wanted to quit many times, but you are on a girl's trip and they won't let you quit. You finally make it. You are hot. You are at the waterfall and you know you need to walk through, except they say you have to jump. You are a little scared, you don't know what's on the other side, and it looks dark, but you were told what was waiting on the other side was worth every second of fear, and chafing of the thighs. So you have a choice: you can either stay where you are and let everyone else go or you can jump through the waterfall, which will be so refreshing. You remember this '5, 4, 3, 2, 1' thing you had heard recently and JUMP! Either that, or the tour guide kindly nudged you! You come above water and you see this breathtaking view: a white sandy beach, chairs, and delicious adult beverages are waiting. They give you a voucher for massages and the most amazing food. Then they say, "We took care of everything for five days, including your kids. Just relax."

Oh my, after confirming this was indeed not a scam and you were not about to die, you do what all moms would do if you have a day alone. You take a nap.

And you think, "What if I would not have jumped? I would still be waiting for everyone else, sweaty and anxious because I was alone. I would probably be doubting everything about the trip and life up to this point. I am sure I would be seriously upset and mad at everyone that left me alone. I would be a mess."

We miss out when we make choices, or choose not to do anything out of fear. This happens because our mess has taken over; we can't even see clearly enough to know what we need to do.

I don't want you to focus on what you have missed in life or how things could and would have been different. There's no point to that at all except to keep you in your mess.

What I want you to know is the truth. You are precious, you are capable, you are worthy, no matter what! (1 John 4:4)

| **No More Hot Mess Mantra:** |
| I am precious, I am accepted, I am enough. |
| I am a treasured woman. |

No matter what choice you have made, His love for you is not based on your performance, but on His perfect surrender at the cross. When you are saved, it is not because of what you can do, but what he can and will do through you.

You have not missed out yet, but you can.

It's time to fold the laundry sister, catch your dream, love on your hubby a bit, and quit using your genetic makeup to keep you from a happy and healthy life.

No More Hotmess

What is one thing that you KNOW God is asking you to do right now?

I look back on life in just the last few years and first He asked me to leave healthcare. Oh, did I ever fight this. It was such a crazy and farfetched idea, but God clearly asked me to do it. I had done things my way and it was not fulfilling and the Lord was asking me to let Him show me what he wanted. But it took me two years for me to be completely obedient. During the time between when I know the Lord was calling me towards His plan and away from mine, I knew I was being disobedient. I was scared, I was confused, I doubted. Bottom line is I was disobedient. And if God is calling you to something, you do not have to not have to waste another minute in disobedience.

It took me months to walk in BELIEF and trust with this book.

What is the Lord asking you to do?

What are your reasons for not doing it?

I personally have found that if I am being a bit lazy with one thing, it often influences me to be lazy in other areas. If I eat crappy, then, well, I don't want to exercise either. But if I am exercising, then I want to eat better. Do you see a pattern in your life of how you do some things (like not do the laundry or with healthy habits) is usually how you end up doing most other things?

I have shared that I started reading and writing Scripture daily a few years ago now. After about a year of this, I also started reading Christ-focused books, something I never had any interest in or felt would help me. I have to say that I have learned so much by being open to other's perspectives and tips. I am so thankful for other women sharing their hearts. One of the books I read spoke about declaring truth and speaking your truth into existence, much like affirmations. Even though you might not feel them, what you speak about you bring about.

This is why when you speak negatively of yourself or situations, most often this is the exact reality you live. Kind of like the boy who cried wolf, except we do this all the time. We can worry ourselves sick. We know that if we speak life-giving, positive things to ourselves, something chemically changes in our brain.

So this author suggested we write a declaration for ourselves and start affirming it over our lives daily. When I was in a very dark place in my life and when I was confused, I was not understanding what the Lord was doing. I was lost. I needed Jesus. This declaration has been one of the most impactful things for me, so I wanted to make sure to share it with you. I have mine printed out and say it out loud, declaring God's truth over my life.

I want to share it in hopes that you will re-write it and make it your own. Then print and say yours out loud along with writing your affirmation, Scriptures, and gratitude, daily.

Chapter 7

Cheneil's (<u>Insert your name</u>) Declaration of Truth

I declare that breakthroughs are coming in my life, sudden bursts of Your goodness, God. Not a trickle. Not a stream. A flood of healing. A flood of wisdom. A flood of favor. I am a breakthrough person and I choose to live as breakthrough minded. I am expecting you, oh God, to overwhelm me with your goodness and amaze me with your favor. I am ready to receive your continued blessings and be filled with your presence.

Because I have your power in you, oh God, I am wrapped in your unfailing love and grace. I know that I am a treasured woman. Jesus, you are standing behind the rejection and negative voices I hear from Satan with your arms open wide open, waiting to embrace and enfold me in the security of your truth. Your truth is that I am precious, I am accepted, I am enough. No matter what! No matter what choices I have made and often make, your love is not based on my performance. Your love is based on your perfect surrender at the cross.

But I know that I have to choose this love and walk in your truth for it to make a difference in how I journey through life. I choose you, your love, and your way, oh God. I will walk in your truth.

Jesus, thank you for reminding me to hold on to what you say about me. I know that your words are the truth of who you are and the essence of what I am created to be. I know that you share your truth with me to help me believe. And when I believe, the truth with set me free.

John 8:32

Chapter 8

The Transformation Project

This is the part of the book that I have to talk lovingly and frankly with you because I care about you. And maybe you need permission or maybe you need some tough love or maybe you just need me to show you some things for you to use later when your hotness hits the fan and starts controlling your life. Whichever category you are in, let's go there.

One thing I have learned through my time as a nurse practitioner and lifestyle coach is that there's a lot of searching and looking, listening and reading, hoping, a lot of couch sitting, wine drinking and chocolate eating (and trust me, I have and still do my fair share), even praying and begging, but often there is little action.

Most of the things that we desperately search for are right in front of us, but we choose to sit behind the mess and NOT act. And I, too, fell into this! Not only once, but twice. Month after month until every ounce of my life and inner spirit was impacted by what I wholeheartedly believe was my disobedience.

So today, I take action!

You are holding this book and reading these God-inspired words because I know God's truth and I made a decision to STOP allowing the enemy to win. Not because I don't still have doubts or fear, but because I know that my God is capable of much more than I am. The Lord has things to say through me and He is literally waiting. He's been waiting for months for me to just let Him do what he wants to do in and through me. He NEVER needs perfection, he just needs us to be willing to open our minds and hearts and move our hands and feet.

If I can be honest, when I finally stop with all the craziness, the excuses, the nonsense, and crap I have been telling myself, it's pretty liberating to see things for what they really are. I am able to see ME for who I really am, because now I can take action.

Be the Hammer

What if your bold faith and courageous action lead to a generational shift of change?

I honestly remember the first time that I hit a softball over the fence! I remember the field in Kilgore, Tx and the feeling after doing it. I think I still have the game ball. I'm not sure why I still have it, but maybe it's to remind me where I came from, or to remind me of life before I started doubting myself, before I worried about others. Hammer, that was the nickname I was given for most of my elementary school days. I grew up as a competitive athlete; winning was in my blood. I was a hard worker and not winning or not rising to the occasion was never an option. Even in college when I barely passed classes or when I failed my nurse practitioner certifications exams multiple times, quitting or saying "I can't" (although something I felt like I needed to do,) was never an option. I had something to prove and it was that I could do hard things. I always felt a sense of being overwhelmed, thinking, "What if I failed?" But it never kept me from doing what I started or believed I could do. Yes, I hammered it over the fence, but this mentality became something I used for most everything else I did. Show up and go for it. Hammer your way to the top.

But let me tell you, when I felt the Lord calling me to write this book I thought, "O Lord. Here we go again. This is big, this is beyond me. I don't know if I am up for failing again." But I agreed anyway. I believed that I had some things to share and I believed that God would also show up on these pages and be life-changing for someone. But when I would sit down to write, I would feel the enemy sitting next to me, distracting me from all angles. He would be pushing me down, disrupting my marriage and my ministry, causing me to doubt my husband's love and my worth as a coach, just to name a few. The enemy often used EVERY OUNCE of my day to target doubt, fear, and confusion. So you can imagine that the enemy didn't want me to sit down and write a meaningful, thought-provoking, truth-giving book for women who need a breakthrough, like I needed. And I admit, I was letting him win.

At the end of the day, every day that I didn't take action where the Lord has called me to take action, I was not only being disobedient, but one of my sisters were missing out on hope and love. My frustration and disappointment in myself grew. When we don't do something we know we are supposed to do, even though we think that not doing it is easier, we are actually creating inner turmoil that really doesn't make it easier at all. And although I thought I was disappointing God, like maybe you think you are doing, that is not true. I was not disappointing God. He didn't love me any less, he doesn't love you any less, but the people affected by me not acting was impacting far more than just me.

We know that God doesn't really need us, but He chose us to live out YOUR unique purpose. YES. He is choosing to use you and needs your mind, your heart, your hands and feet. (Matthew 22:37) So when we say NO, when we allow fear, doubt, shame, frustration, confusion, and lies dictate our life, God does not get to use us. YOU, my dear sister, have specific purposes that the LORD needs you to do, like being the mother to your children. YOU were created for THEM and them for YOU! Being the wife to your husband, YOU were created for HIM and him for YOU!

If I was not willing to get up and FIGHT BACK like I have done since the "hammer days," asking people to pray for me and with me to send Satan back to hell and away from my mind and my heart, you wouldn't be reading this. You would not see truth, hear truth, and quite possibly not step into your BOLD FAITH like we are created to do. You see, if I don't do what I am called to do, I miss out, and thousands of women miss out. If you decide not to rise up, to be the hammer in your own life and you do not act on your bigger purpose, people miss out.

I decided that I cannot sit back and allow the enemy to continue to win because if I did, then YOU would miss out on His love, His grace, His mercy and the TRUTH OF WHO YOU ARE AND WHO HE IS! What I know is that my journey of rising up and fighting back is exactly what you need to do, too. We must be willing to do this, to be the hammer in our own lives. Not because we need to go around knocking everything out of the park, but because we need to be ready to do what it takes. I don't know exactly what areas of your life need refining, or renovating, but I do know that it's time!

It's time for you to be the hammer in your own life.

<u>No More Hotmess</u>

You are digging in your heels with something. I know you are. What is it?

What is making you stand back and wait?

What does it mean to you to miss out because you didn't act?

Chapter 8

Chapter 9

It's a ZOO in Here so Might as Well Act like a Monkey

Having two little boys in the house has allowed me to be more aware of animals than I ever thought I would be. From books, countless trips to the zoo, and curious minds, I found myself learning more about animals, too. One of the animals that I am mesmerized with is birds. I think they are amazing for several reasons.

Every time we go to the zoo there is always an "exotic bird sighting." One of the zookeepers shares the story of the bird and there is one particular exhibit where the zookeeper sends the bird off and it always comes back. And then there are other exhibits where the birds are just sitting as the zookeeper is talking. I have always been amazed that these birds just obey and stay. They are literally free to fly away, but they choose to stay.

Well, we know that this is because most birds in the zoo setting have been conditioned to believe that they don't have freedom. As the birds are growing, they are trained to obey, kind of like our children, who could walk out of the house at any time, but they don't. The birds are conditioned and they just believe that they cannot leave. This is why the parrots stay put at the zoo entrance, the birds at the exhibits obey and don't fly off.

The bird feels safe and comfortable. If only they realized that an open sky was right in front of them, that freedom was right there. But they don't.

When I think about these birds and even kids, I also think about the things that are dictating our lives without us even realizing it things that we are allowing to control us that either don't even exist or the things that we have allowed to completely control our entire life. These birds are trained and conditioned to stay put, basically in bondage, bound to their environment their entire life. Truthfully they believe the lie that they have no choice and live their entire life under this limitation and lie. But they don't even know any different. I think this is the most astonishing thing and one that leaves me unbelievably thankful that I am not a bird or elephant or other zoo animals for that matter. But y'all, how often do we live exactly like this? We allow excuses and lies to literally dictate our entire lives, and often we use people and life circumstances as the things that "make us live a certain way."

My husband isn't on the same page as I am, so when he decides to support me, then maybe I will get on board, too.

My kids need too much of me. They get up too early and they don't allow me the time I need for me and to get important things done.

My parents have always been so negative and critical. This is how they are, I get it from them, and it will probably never change.

The demands on my life, kids, work, and house require all of my time and there is none left for me.

I don't have the money, nor will I ever be able to afford that marriage conference or business coach.

Chapter 9

If I lost the weight, I would be happier and life would be better.

If we all sat for a few minutes just thinking about the week again, I guarantee that the first thing that starts going through all of our minds are negative lies and excuses.

And y'all, what we think about, what we focus on, becomes our reality. If you are constantly thinking of why you can't, what you don't have, all that needs to be different, then guess what? You guessed it… your life becomes not good enough. You become not good enough, all because of the thoughts you are thinking.

I am not saying that some of these things are not true or are not our reality, but what I am saying is that most often, we are allowing a lie to keep us coming back to our "comfort zone," even if this place is miserable. And we keep coming back day after day, week after week, year after year. We have come so accustomed to this place, it feels and seems part of who we are. So much so, that we are justifying our negative thoughts, action or our inaction.

Now hear me. I am not discrediting terrible living conditions, lack of support, or lack of love. I understand that we all have basic needs that need to be met and if not met, it is very difficult to NOT fall into survival mode. And if this is your situation, please get help.

Is it really OK to give someone, other than our heavenly father, so much power over your life that they literally control your action, or inactions? Is this really OK?

> ## No More Hot Mess Mantra:
> ### I AM FREE-
> ### Galatians 5:13

Alone, we are powerless. Alone we are controlled by FEAR: False Evidence Appearing Real. But sister, we are called to freedom. (Galatians 5:13)

Freedom that does not come from our husbands, kids, career, a perfect weight, perfect life, more money, or more things. This is freedom that can only be found in Christ, sister.

I imagine when our Heavenly Daddy looks down on us and sees the stuff holding us back, He is upset, just heartbroken. I imagine His heart is aching after relentlessly pursuing an intimate relationship with us each and every day just to see us settle for bondage. I believe that because we choose so many other things instead of Him, it grieves him. I am confident that living as a hotmess is not the kind of life he would have for us sister. Not at all.

Take a second to think about the birds of the sky, particularly those in a controlled environment.

Think about your life. And no, I am not saying visualize yourself as a bird! I am asking you to find the comfortable places in your life, the places that you tend to come back to because that's just what you are used to doing. Let them surface. Allow yourself to see them. So often, we have been living a certain way for so long that we don't even realize that there's a different possibility or reality.

Chapter 9

Where do I start…. my husband.

I was depending on him to make me feel worthy, approved, and enough… I looked to him instead of Jesus. No one on this earth deserves that kind of pressure. And no one on this earth should have that much power over our lives either. Y'all, I was constantly setting myself up for failure. If I weigh my worth on what someone else can do for me, I will simply ALWAYS be disappointed.

Let me say, marriage is sacred. It is a kingdom covenant to be taken very seriously and when entering into it, we have vowed to sacrificially and selflessly love. To enter marriage is to join in a divine partnership, displaying the image of Christ and the Church. Yes. That is how serious marriage is. It is ridiculous for me or anyone else to think that our partner should 100% complete us. They are a gift, a partner. But they cannot and should not be our completer, nor should they be our reason not to live in obedience.

It's the same thing with our kids, money or things, or even addictions. God is the only one who can and will ever be able to complete us. I could have allowed my husband to literally STOP me in my tracks. And some days it did. But I would not be writing this today if I would have allowed lies that Satan uses to create separation and isolation. I do believe that so much of what we feel are impossibilities in our lives is warfare. But I also believe that people and things can be this place that we go to try to fix us or the problem. Many of you may be living in a hindering situation that seems impossible to break free from. And breaking free does not mean to walk away. I am saying to release control and decide that the thing or the person no longer has control over you or should keep you from taking action in your life. Breaking free is to live in FREEDOM!

I know that it is easy to be the victim, to not do anything, and blame yourself or them or things. But here's the deal, God did not create us to be tied down, to simply be and die wishing and hoping for different. Are you kidding me? He is pursuing us because he loves us, He thinks we are so unbelievably amazing, and He has some very special things He wants us to be a part of with him.

So when we are allowing things to hold us back, not only can we NOT run to Jesus freely to receive His embrace, but we miss some really amazing things, like inner peace, love and grace. We all have a choice. We can choose to stay in our conditioned state of fake controlled discomfort, or we can choose freedom. We can either live on the basis of what we think we can or cannot do, or LIVE IN FREEDOM based on what God said He would do through us. What God is calling us to, in our marriages, our callings, our everyday things, he will equip and sustain.

> **No More Hot Mess Mantra:**
> I am fully equipped-
> Philippians 4:19

We have all we need. (Philippians 4:19; 2 Peter 1:3) He gives us strength and love. (Isaiah 40:20; Jeremiah 31:3) He said, in Him, we can do the things that seem impossible, but He will do them. (Matthew 19:26) He said he will take our hand and walk with us. (Psalm 73:23)

No More HotMess

So what is it that is controlling your life? What things come to mind when talking about comforts. Most of us have a few, so don't think you are alone.

When I started processing through the strongholds in my life, the places that I found myself continuing to come back to because they were my "safe place" the place I thought was comfortable, but kept me continually uncomfortable, it took a while. Honestly, I have had to deal with each one a little differently, and this continues to be true with new things today.

When I feel out of control, when I feel like I am being drawn back to the places that causes so much discontentment, frustration, and even pain, the places that make me feel like I can't see straight or breathe, I have learned some tips that will help you, too.

These are a few TRUTH TIPS:

- Stop and ask God for help. Out loud, "HELP ME GOD!" YES! I KNOW! It is a Sunday School answer, but truthfully, we are functioning in pure independence and self-sufficiency most of the time. It is the same response I have when I am feeling overwhelmed and I know it is the enemy. "Get out of here! In the name of Jesus leave my head and heart NOW!" The enemy knows that we are striving and searching for love, acceptance, appreciation, and most of the time, it is JESUS that we need. And He is right here waiting. We need Him to comfort us, to love us, to guide us, reassure us. Expecting others to do this is simply not realistic or fair most of the time.

- Drop the assumptions from all sides and find your focus. Most often, when I was allowing my husband to frustrate me or hurt me, it was from a place of need. Of loneliness. I needed him to meet some sort of need and most often he didn't even know this. Do not assume.

- Roll into His arms. Here is the bottom line sister. We cannot allow other people, circumstances, our past, or these places and feelings that seem comfortable but are not good or healthy to run our lives. I wholeheartedly believe that God would never want us to live in a state of being stuck forever. Being stuck or tied down means we don't want Him to use us or proclaim His power. When we willingly stay stuck, we are assuming all power, and ultimately choosing a false sense of control over our own life. You, my dear sister, were created for so much more than this!

What would your life look like in 30 days if you were able to let yourself go, to live in freedom? Allow God to come in and clean things up and help you see YOUR TRUE SELF AND TRUE FREEDOM you have in Him?

Remember, just as the free birds of the sky, those not in a zoo are free and unfettered, not tied down to a job description. They live careless in the care of God. And you, my dear sister, count far more to God than birds (Matthew 6:26). Not only are the birds of the air cared for by God, He provided them with food from insects and shelter in the trees, and these are birds! How much more does God care about us? This truly amazes me.

No More Hot Mess

Let's do some work.

Take a second to fill in the blanks.

I HAVE BEEN ALLOWING _____ TO HOLD ME DOWN AND HOLD ME BACK.

This makes me feel_____.

Today, I am cutting free of _____ and feel _____. I AM _____.

. . . .

Why is the right thing so stinkin' hard? Because it matters. I used to think (and would even have people say), that if it is hard, then that just means the Lord is trying to tell you not to do it. Oh, oh, sister. One of the biggest lessons I have learned is that if it seems impossible, if it seems too hard to handle, then you should lift your head and hold on tight because God is calling you out into the storm. If it weren't difficult then you wouldn't need Jesus. You couldn't handle it on your own. So anytime you are tempted to walk away, say "Forget it," and assume that Jesus is closing the door, (even though you know deep in your heart it's what you should do), remember that you are never expected to do the hard stuff alone. Your obedience in that hard thing might bring you to the exact place you have been begging for.

What if His promises are right on the other side of your obedience?

Chapter 9

Chapter 10

The Butterfly Effect

**All thing are working together for my good-
Ephesians 3:20-21**

I need my bug catcher. NOW! Mom, where is it?"

My son would cry, whine, and cry some more. "Where is it?"
he frantically asked, then explained, "I need to help these
bugs by gathering them to be close to their family. So,
amongst all the crying and whining, I walked over to the toy
chest and, right in front of him, on top of all the toys, just
within reach... was the bug catcher. A few minutes later, he
runs over and says, "Look mommy. They are all together as
a family. We saved them." I look down and see a ridiculous
number of flies that he had snatched with his hand, because
that is the Texas boy thing to do in the summer, I guess. I
am still wondering how a 3-year-old caught flies like that. But
there they were, a huge family reunion of flies. I laughed, a
bit disgusted, wondering where those things had been, and
my heart was overwhelmed with the sweetness of this little
boy.

A few days later he is asking again for a bug catcher, except
this time it's for a butterfly that had landed on the sandpit in
the backyard. In his three-year-old snatchy skills, he caught
the butterfly along with a cocoon. I had no idea what to
expect, and honestly didn't think there was anything in the
cocoon. A few days later, we saw a small hole in the cocoon.

You could actually see the butterfly, and for several hours we could see it struggle to squeeze its body through the tiny hole. Then it stopped, as if it couldn't go further. My other son, the proclaimed animal doctor, wanted to help. He pulled away the remaining bits of cocoon. I asked him to just leave it alone for a bit so we wouldn't traumatize the butterfly like they had done to many roly polies before. So, like all boys, they were immediately distracted by something else in the yard. A few hours later, they checked in on the butterfly, but its body was swollen and wings shriveled. We watched and I certainly didn't know what to do. We expected the wings would enlarge and expand enough to support the body at any time.

Neither happened! In fact, the butterfly wasn't able to fly. According to Google, when you remove the cocoon, it actually prevents the natural process of helping the butterfly fly. The hole in the cocoon and the struggle required by the butterfly to get through the opening was a way of forcing the fluid from the body into the wings so that it would be ready for flight.

Y'ALL. The struggle was required to fly. I didn't know any of this about butterflies so I learned a lot, but then I realized that if God cares so much about a butterfly that he would place a struggle in its life to help it become what it is created to be, to fly, do you not think that our heavenly father might care about us? I think about the hurt, the pain from our past, the struggle with finances, the coping we do to deal with the stress, and all the hotmess, y'all.

We all have it! We all have something.

And quite frankly, even if you are moving forward in a direction you want to go, your kids are healthy, your marriage is healthy, you are rocking your dream life, you are in your best health ever, there's still gonna be something! It's called LIFE. For some of us this stuff involves mental, emotional struggles, some are injuries, money, family member issues.... There is always going to be something.

Sister!!!! Hear me, because I am serious. There is no perfect rainbows-and-unicorns stress-free life.

And if God needs a butterfly to struggle to come to LIFE, then I think the same is even more true of us. Through our struggle we need Him. He wants us to see this, understand this, and let Him be our source through it all. And if you are still wanting to sit in your trauma, pain, struggle, confusion, frustration, and all the reasons why you can't, shouldn't and probably won't ever, I can't sit here and say that's OK. I validate your circumstances and your pain, but I still think you have to look up instead of continuing to circle in the mess.

What if the struggles that you have been through and are going through right now are not something to use as blame, to be frustrated with, or to be confused about. (Not to say that they aren't at first.) What if your struggles are opportunities to lean in? An invitation to come sit a while and be embraced by our creator so that He can show you His love and grace in and through it?

What if your struggle is exactly what YOU need to experience who you are created to be? What if your struggle and the journey to overcome is exactly how God is using your mess to make a miracle?

As hard as it can be, as lonely, frustrating, and confusing it can be, your struggles do not get the power to control you! Your struggles do not define you! Your struggles do not get to hold you down.

Not only did the butterfly have to pry open the hole, he had to keep coming back to pry it open. It wasn't easy; I am sure it was frustrating. And getting through the hole was a bit painful, right? But the butterfly had to endure this to live fully, to fly freely. Just like the butterfly, if we just sat back and hoped, doubted, lived in fear of the pain and overwhelmed at how long it could take, we miss out on what is occurring as part of the growing process. What if, like the butterfly, we are trying to omit the life giving-process we need to go through by prematurely stopping the things in our lives that we need to experience, so that we are not fully developed? Matured. Sister, if every butterfly did what the majority of us do: worry, complain, sit back, and do NOTHING, there would be less pollination for plants, vegetables, fruit, as well as less food for other animals and less beauty for us to enjoy. Think about how many things are affected by a butterfly.

Think about how many people and things are affected by us not being willing to stand up and willing to RISE UP to fight the good fight.

It comes down to why in the world would these butterflies willingly do this? Every single one of them goes through this process. Just like childbirth, women endure knowing it is going to be miserable.

But they BELIEVE. It's not that some are "stronger than others," or more disciplined, or have better this or that... they believe the process is worth it.

NoMoreHotMESS

What is your most impactful struggle right now? The one that seems to be affecting most areas of your life? The one that you keep thinking about?

Do you believe your struggle is worth the struggle?

What are you wrapped in? What's holding you back?

- that you will never be loved again
- that you will never be disciplined enough
- that you will never be enough
- that you will never be smart enough to live your dream
- that _____
- that _____

God knows what you are going through. He does not like to see us in pain or to see us struggle. But he also knows that this is LIFE. Y'all, He knows that we will struggle. (John 16:33) I know it's easier to try to avoid any struggle and it makes more sense to prevent it. I get it. But can there be purpose in your pain? Could there be a miracle birthed out of your mess?

Could the pain, the hardship, and the pressures be part of the growing process to create maturity in your faith? (James 1:1)

Could it be that the journey to fully trusting is what creates an unshakable reassurance and peace that ultimately minds the void and the pain? (John 16:33)

Could it be that our cocoon of discomfort is our connection to our creator? He lived a blameless life, yet endured much suffering, even death on a cross for us to have freedom. Could it be that our cocoon is making us human, in need of a savior? (1 Peter 2:23-25)

As much as we don't like to talk about handicaps, could it be that our pain, our weakness, our cocoon, is a gift reminding us of God's power in us? (2 Corinthians 12:7-10)

Chapter 11

Do you Believe?

When the Lord asked me to write this book, he told me that he wanted me to write a book about discipline. WHAT? Discipline? So yes, I waited until the end to share that because, sister, let's be real, If I shared about discipline at the beginning, would you still be reading? I am not dumb. Although the enemy often tries to convince me that I am, but I am learning that this is a lie. But hello, who the heck wants to read a book on disciple? YOU DO! Trust me, because this is so important. When I think about the word discipline, I think about staying committed to what I said I was going to do. (Matthew 5:37) For me, doing what I committed to do has pretty much been a way of life for me. It's part of the way I was wired, but it's also a desire to please myself and God. But I am just like you, and when life gets messy, and busy I realize that I have a choice whether to show up, and for some reason, I decide not to. We are comfortable with comfort. With ok. With normal. Or maybe we are afraid of the uncomfortable. Or maybe there's so much stuff in our lives that it seems impossible to put ourselves on the list. Or maybe there's a little part of us that has actually decided that we don't need to be on our to-do list anymore.

> **No More Hot Mess Mantra:**
> God's grace was enough and all that
> mattered-
> 2 Corinthians 12:9

When life gets messy, most of the time, this mess ends up mattering most. We ALL have messy lives. Every single one of us. We all have "too much on our plates," we all have many hats we wear, we all have many obligations, we all have a list that never ends, we all have the house that constantly needs to be cleaned or picked up, or the pile of laundry that never gets folded. But why is it that some of us RISE UP, commit to things and stay committed, create discipline with healthy routines, make themselves a priority, don't look at quitting as an option, and some of us don't?

Does it really come down to disciple?

It was dark, and I was exhausted and sobbing. I needed someone to hold me and tell me I was worthy and loved and that my identity was in Christ and only Christ. (1 Peter 2:9; John 1:12) I needed to know that God's grace was enough and all that mattered. (2 Corinthians 12:9) I needed to know that my performance would not matter in heaven, but only my love for others and my obedience to His calling.

I was confused. (1 Corinthians 14:33)

I had finished a basketball game soulfully upset with myself. For some reason, this time was worse than others. I had missed some free throws that ultimately didn't cause us to lose, but it definitely didn't help us win. I was so disappointed in myself that I came home and proceeded to cry and shoot free throws for at least an hour in the dark. I remember my dad coming home and walking over to me saying, "What are you doing?" And then I don't remember much after that. He could have said more things, but I was so disappointed and disgusted that all that was going through my head was what a failure I was and how I will never measure up. I had started to believe I was less than, less capable, less pretty, and less smart. Oh, all the lies that were swarming in my teenage head. And the blame just kept coming. I had no idea that from that moment on I would base my worth on how well I performed and base my love for myself and the love from my heavenly father on how well I lived out this life.

You see, lies that started creeping in long before I even realized what they meant or realized how profoundly they would haunt me started to impact so much of me and my life. I developed a belief system about myself that was all wrong and twisted. But it was EXACTLY how the enemy works. He intentionally finds ways to lie, steal, cheat and destroy, doing everything he can to keep us from truly understanding who we are and why we exist. (Revelation 12:10) The confusion that you feel right now, the misunderstanding, and the distance, it was never God's plan.

In Christ, there is no confusion, there is no condemnation. (1 Corinthians 14:33; Romans 8:1) There is clarity, there is peace beyond understanding. (Philippians 4:7) There is FREEDOM! (2 Corinthians 3:17) Most of us have no idea what it looks like, feels like, or have even imagined what a life of true freedom in Christ looks like. Call me crazy, but I have barely been able to see past my toes from pregnancies, past my messy house and car, or past a pretend schedule that I make to try and make myself feel better. I get it! Most of us aren't interested in anything that seems like work.

But I want you to understand truth! The truth is, you need to quit your hotmess life. Crush your name badge and put on a brand new one, a badge that you can truly be proud of.

(Ephesians 4:22-24) Change does not come down to you being disciplined or a better Christian.

It comes down to the work of the holy spirit. It comes down to belief. A belief in Jesus AND a belief that he can use you.

You were made to be unstoppable!

I want you to be empowered with a swift kick of love to your behind. Listen, we all struggle with something: confidence, understanding, feeling overwhelmed, distractions, fear, shame, and doubt. We are all a mess.

But I want you to know that you know that you know that you are LOVED so, so much. (1 John 3:1) You are not bound to your mess. You truly have everything you need in you: the spirit! He is in you! (1 John 4:4) You are 100% compatible with Jesus and you can completely ROCK your life, sister because He is in you. If I can change my heart and my mind towards our God, towards myself, and towards my place in this world, by golly, you can too!

I was on my own journey of finding the real Cheneil a few years back, and part of this journey was discovering WHO I was, whether I really wanted to tap into God's power in my life and let him do his thing, and what I really wanted out of this life, too.

God has needed me to travel down MY road of pain, frustration, loneliness, and feeling overwhelmed. He never ever said our lives would be easy, or on a silver platter, or a quick fix, all the things we all want if we are being honest. But my journey has been very much about God revealing to me HIS story of redemption, love, grace, and of an unending embrace that I believe I have longed for since I was a little girl.

He wanted to show me that not only does he love me so much that he died for me and thinks so highly of me that he invited me to be part of His story, but I know he continues to want me to see just what he is truly capable of doing in and through me. I believe that he longs to show us that we are miraculously made. (Isaiah 43:1) On the outside I showed up and performed pretty darn good for years, but on the inside, I was extremely selfish and insecure, so much so that no matter how hard I tried or how many awards, education, and recognition I received, I still felt empty and not good enough. I used my physical talents in high school and my hard work ethic in college to "rise above" and get advanced degrees, but what I found when I landed my first real job, real relationship, and real problems was that I had very little belief in myself and very little faith or trust in my God. I would never deny that the Lord was completely involved in every single aspect of my life, but I rarely even looked up to ask for guidance or if the path I was choosing was what he wanted for me. I just made a decision and did it, hoping that it would make me feel better and give me the peace, worth, and happiness I longed for.

Over the years I started discovering that not only was I in a place that I didn't really want to be, I had put up many walls around me out of fear and insecurities. I didn't want to fail, and I would go to extremes to avoid it. You have probably been here, so afraid of failing that you are extremely hesitant to give yourself the permission to do the hard stuff.

So I am giving you permission to fail and fall into the arms of Jesus. With whatever you have going on that seems too much, from whatever it is that you want to walk away from, lean in. Instead of giving up or walking away, this time lean in, fall into Jesus. Where he brought you, he will sustain you. (Philippians 4:13)

No More Hotmess

When was the last time you said, I CAN?

Maybe that's getting up earlier to have some time with Jesus and to take control of your day instead of letting it control you. Maybe that's adding a sweat sesh into your day, knowing it might stink during, but you will be proud when you are done. Maybe that's scheduling date nights because you believe your marriage matters. Maybe that's connecting with a counselor.

What is it? How will you fight the mess? What action will you take today?

The reality is, YOU can! Instead of limiting your belief and allowing fears, and quite frankly, laziness to win, what if our new language was YES YOU CAN and you were empowered by a NEW CREATION mindset that not only gave you new life, but allowed you to experience things and feelings that you might not have ever felt or knew were possible?

As a mom, we already do so much. You are a powerhouse, a rockstar. YOU ARE! The cooking, cleaning, caring for kids, schedule, and career are just a few things I know that you are juggling. You are amazing and you are already doing so much, so when it comes to YOU, and doing what you need to do to live your best life, quit saying you can't.

Finding Fearless; your new way

I just want you to know that this time, YOU AREN'T TURNING AWAY!

I AM NOT GOING TO LET YOU!

Instead of looking at all you haven't done as failure and defeat, what if you looked at it as an opportunity to not use your own strength but a supernatural strength and experience; the red velvet cupcake life. His good life, a life where we don't have to let fear, anxiety, feeling overwhelmed, and our past dictate all of our action. A life where we don't honor the hotmess, and as a matter of fact, we refuse to live this way.

What if the very thing that the holy spirit is prompting you to do is the VERY thing that will allow you to have freedom in your life? The kind of freedom that actually lets God do His job? What if you started to feel and experience victory instead of defeat? What if you started to see you for who you are and what God was capable of?

Instead of I can't _____.

I can _____.

I shouldn't _____.

I will _____.

Erase the Lies and Affirm His Truth

Fear of not measuring up. The only thing I am measured up against is my belief in Jesus.

Fear of being abandoned by _____. I have never been forgotten or abandoned.

Fear of being criticized or judged by _____. Instead, God is my only judge and I will not fear man.

Fear of letting _____ down. I will never let down God.

Fear of the pain of _____. I will not forget the pain and I don't have to, but I will not let the pain dictate how I live.

What are some other places in your heart or head that you need to rewrite?

What are they? List them here or even just share them with God.

What are you afraid of?

_____

_____

_____

_____

_____

_____

_____

_____

_____

_____

Then spend a few minutes affirming truth. Here are some "I am" statements. Affirmations. New Creation Declarations. Feel free to add to them, too. Don't skip this sister, because HERE is where freedom starts.

I will not live on the basis of what I can do, but on what God said he will do through me.

I am a treasured woman.

God's love is not based on my performance.

I choose LOVE.

I choose to walk in FAITH, not to be held down my fear.

I am enough, because He who is greater than the world is within me.

I choose to live out his truth because I know the truth will set me free.

I am highly favored by God.

I am unapologetically illuminating the talents and gifts that God has intentionally given me (Romans 12:6)

I am anchored in the wisdom, anointed discernment, and love of God. (John 15:5-8)

His glory zone exists outside my comfort zone.

Whatever I ask, if I believe, I will receive. (Mark 11:24)

I am available and ready to do Your Work. (Isaiah 6:8)

I am a beautiful masterpiece.

I have a peace that surpasses all understanding. (Philippians 4:7)

I am a new creation. (2 Corinthians 5:17)

Chapter 12

Just Pull the Band-Aid

Sometimes we have to be ripped of the VERY thing we are finding our identity in to see the majesty of God. Separating from these things is often required to actually see Him and experience Him.

It was a cold January at 12 noon, and I was in the counselor's office for the first time. He allowed me to share my story, and in such love, kept asking questions and more questions. I had no idea why or what he was going to do with the information, but I was glad to just share things from my past that I didn't even realize were relevant to my life–Towards the end, he asked about a typical day in the life of Cheneil. So, I proceeded to share. I have a 3-year-old and an 18-month-old, I work as a nurse practitioner on rotating shifts, and I am growing an online business. I work on ME before kids and I work on my business in my car before work and after work! I am exhausted all the time. My marriage, well, we are here. And the question that always makes me want to slap someone came out of my counselors' mouth: "Do you ever rest?" UMMM, what do you mean, do I rest? I don't rest. He laughed. And then he said it again. "But do you rest?" He rephrased the comment or said it again because I missed what he was saying. I was still confused, and he could tell because he said, "You don't stop, do you?" And I broke. Hearing myself tell him all that I was doing, yet still feeling dissatisfied and disappointed with myself, brought me to sobbing tears. I won't measure up. I won't be good enough. I am not enough, no matter what I do. I have a lot of things in place like an endless to-do list so that I get to check off a lot of boxes, but at the end of the day, I still fail.

I had labeled myself as a failure because literally every day, that is how I felt. Up until this point, instead of the hotness badge, I was wearing the failure badge. I felt I was always disappointing God and could never measure up, and somehow this also translated into questioning God's love, not understanding God grace or favor, and blaming myself for the lack of blessings in my life. These thoughts were all deeply rooted on my performance. It was a vicious cycle of defeat, and let me tell you, Satan had a stronghold in this area of my life. I was miserable. After the Lord called me away from my nurse practitioner career and I was living out my passion and dream as a full-time lifestyle coach, I found myself in a similar dilemma of LONG nights, pressing into all the activities of growing a business. Once again, I started to feel a bit shameful and less worthy. Surely God was not pleased with me, and that is why things are not picking up or growing. I must not be doing something right, he must not approve of me or what I am doing. Things got hard y'all. *You will never be good enough for Me to use you* are the things I started to hear.

The dream in your heart: speaking, serving others on a ranch with your family, writing, adopting a child, leading medical missions, being a vessel of love and truth, Cheneil, it is all made up. No one needs you or wants your help. You are not worthy, you are not capable, and I cannot use you. Your parents do not support you, your husband will never support you and love you like you need him to, and by the way, your kids are being neglected and you are not a good mother. All the time spent trying to grow a business and ministry is pushing them away and soon they will see you are not a good mom. This is exactly what the enemy was speaking over me and telling me over and over and over for days. I believed the lies. Just like you. I would believe them and this would dictate how I was living. I was a complete and utter hotmess.

One minute I found myself overwhelmed with gratitude getting to meet so many amazing women online, getting to live out my passion and purpose every day, getting to take my kids to school and pick them up, getting to put them to bed, and doing so many things that for years I thought I would never be able to do. I am thankful. Then the next minute I would be overwhelmed with mistakes, with insecurities, doubts, and guilt.

I was a mess, and quite honestly, I was living like a hotmess. My entire life. My mental health, my physical health, my house. My thoughts were constantly all over the place. My morning routine wasn't happening. I was allowing little things to slide with every part of my life. And when I sat down to write, my mind was cluttered. I couldn't seem to get my thoughts to come together.

I was a complete mess.

I couldn't think clearly, I couldn't get my thoughts together. And I was starting become "ok" with some of it. I had been saying, "It's ok Cheneil. You can sleep a little longer. It's ok Cheneil, you can have another dessert or drink. It's ok Cheneil." I was giving myself a lot of "grace." But I was miserable. I knew this was not what I needed to do and how I needed to live. I knew that God's grace was sufficient and I didn't need to add any of mine to the mix. The spirit was nudging me with discontentment with all the mess, but I continued to try and cover it up.

But the truth of the matter is, within this messy life that I was living, one day I realized that I did not have to be a mess. Just because my life was messy, which is true for all of us, I did not have to live like a mess. I am not messy. I am not created to be a mess. The Lord doesn't delight in me when I am constantly a mess. Sister, I love you, but God cannot use you if you are constantly a mess. We can't hear him and we can't see the amazing things he is trying to do right in front of us. We can't make ourselves available to him. We can't hear from him. It's simple, but it's true. And please don't hear me say that you have to be perfect to hear from God and be used by God. NO! That is not at all what I am trying to say. I am saying that we all have messy lives and God is trying to work a miracle out of your mess. But if our hearts, our minds, our bodies, our finances, our marriages, or families and relationships are always a mess and we are not willing to make changes, how can we see what God is trying to do?

Before kids, we were the aunt and uncle who offered to keep our one and two-year-old niece and nephews overnight because we loved these kids and of course we wanted to be the cool aunt and uncle. We loved them like our own, except we could pretend and give them back. But I do remember using these times as a practice run. More so mentally. I remember thinking, "We can do this, maybe we can do this. But we probably should not. I can't do it. I won't love them well enough, I don't have the patience, my work hours won't allow me to be present, and I will lose attention from my husband and he will lose me."

God is not surprised that we want to play by our rules. By nature, because of the fall, we want to indulge in our fleshly, sinful desires. He knows that we want to do what comes easy or we want to feel in control and fix everything. And with this comes the wrath of God. Sister, God knew this! Way, way, way before we were born, God loved us so much (John 3:16) He knew that because of Adam and Eve's selfish decision that we, you and I, would then inherit a sinful nature. This would be our desire or natural state of living. (Genesis 3:15-16)

But guess what, he was NOT OK with this! In His lavish mercy and great, unconditional love for us, he died for us. When he died he took our sin, he took us with Him. Our old self literally died with Him. (Romans 6:4-7)

Take a second to let this sink in. The enemy wants us all to carry around our sin, our fleshly behaviors and desires as though they are still part of us. But sister, this is exactly what the enemy wants you to believe. He wants us to think and feel like we are constantly tied down and in bondage, feeling shameful, guilty, ill-equipped, and insignificant. The enemy wants you to believe that your struggles, your hardships, your sin, is who you are!

But listen to me: This is a lie.

Through Jesus Christ's death on the cross and by God's grace, he saves you. This means your sin, your fleshly desires, literally went to the cross with Him and died (1 Peter 3:18).

He was thinking about YOU when he humbly paid this price. This is no mistake.

And then PRAISE GOD, he did not stay in the grave, but he ROSE from the grave. And when he rose from the dead, you ROSE with Him. When you received Jesus as your savior, your redeemer, this means that He knew that by nature you would struggle with certain things. He knew YOU, all of you and HE made you. And when you said YES to Him, he made you pure, perfect, and righteous (Romans 5:1)

He has His arms reaching out, inviting us to be wrapped in His unfailing love and grace as Jesus Christ sits at the right hand of the Father.

We did not deserve this grace and love, y'all. NOPE. We were born wretched sinners, but when we said "Yes" to Him, he ran to us and continues pursuing us daily. He willingly leaves the 99 to come after us. (Luke 15:1-7) And maybe you are saying, but Cheneil, this addiction, this hard heart, this laziness… I am unclean. I can't change, there is no way that there is such a LOVE as this.

Please know that I understand this is a hard concept to fully grasp.

One of the most profound representations of unconditional love I've experienced has been as a mother. Do you remember me saying that I truly believed that I always had something to prove? That I never felt good enough, that I would blame myself for everything and say no wonder this or that happened? I must not have been working hard enough, or what did I do wrong?

When we start to fully understand and receive this LOVE, a love that encompasses all, endures all, lavishes us unconditionally, we actually start to look at ourselves differently, too.

Ezekiel 36:26-27 "I will give you a new heart and put in you a new spirit; I will remove from you your heart of stone and give you a heart of flesh. And I will put my Spirit in you and move you to follow my decrees and be careful to keep my laws."

2 Corinthians 2:14-16 "But Thanks be to God, who always LEADS US IN TRIUMPHAL PROCESSION IN Christ and through us spreads everywhere the fragrance of the knowledge of him. For we are to God the aroma of Christ among those who are being saved and those who are perishing. To the one we are the smell of death; the other, the fragrance of life. And who is equal to such task?"

Chapter 12

Chapter 13

The Year of the Bad Hair

Think 1990. Still dressing like the 80's, perming our hair and teasing our bangs.

I had just gotten my hair permed for school pictures. So picture a wavy mop look with ratted, frizzy bangs, black leggings, and a purple, slightly off the shoulder top with a little tie to one side. Can you picture it? I can actually remember the smell of that old gym where we took the pictures. Doesn't time just fly, y'all? It is so crazy to look back on life. When I was thinking about that year and that time in my life, I will never forget getting those pictures back, looking at the group picture, and there I was slap in the middle, a foot taller than everyone with my wavy pop and all, smiling from ear to ear. And all of a sudden, I realized that I was different. I was bigger than even the boys in my class and that was strange. I was weird, and I was not normal. I know that is what I saw, because this is what I believed about myself for many years. I became very insecure about my body. Girls are not supposed to be bigger than boys.

And not only do I remember this class book photo taken in that gym, but a few years later, I tried out for junior high cheerleader for the first time and I didn't make it. I was much bigger than the other girls and well, no wonder, I didn't make it. *Had you somehow forgotten that you are not normal? You are bigger and fatter than the other girls, so no wonder you didn't make it. What makes you think you deserve something like that anyway?*

From a very early age, I developed a negative body image. I hated my legs. They are the one part of my body that has literally sent me to my floor crying, many times because nothing could hide them well enough or NOTHING would fit them well enough to make me not feel so subconscious. From the time I really cared or noticed I was growing faster than most other girls, I developed a body image complex. I couldn't explain it and I felt like I couldn't avoid it, but I began to hate my body.

Even when most of the other girls caught up to me, something was still wrong. Something was still not right. I was still fat. My clothes still would not fit right. I would internalize my body insecurities as a problem with me, something that maybe I could control but I wasn't doing enough of.

I remember avoiding mirrors at all cost, was repulsed by my body and found myself in a state of emotional turmoil at times. What would start as a pair of shorts that were my "size" not fitting over my thigh, would end with me crying, not wanting to come out of the dressing room, self-shaming, and hating myself for being the size I was.

My insecurities continued to rage for years, y'all. I wish I could say that it stopped after college or after marriage, when someone accepted me for who I was, but it didn't.

I let my body image disorder take over my thoughts about me, who I was.

I believed that not only was I not attractive, I also brought into my head the thoughts that as a Christian woman, I was not supposed to be confident in my sexuality and confident with myself in the bedroom with my husband. I was always uncomfortable with myself, which translated to me being uncomfortable with him. I didn't think I was OK to be free in the bedroom because I wasn't free in my own mind and heart. I was being controlled by lies that Satan wanted me to stay in bondage to forever.

YES, forever, because my marriage would suffer forever if I continued thinking this way.

Do you hear me?

I was hiding behind a body image disorder, which started when I was in the 5th grade, and this ultimately affected my marriage for years. I wouldn't let it go and we both paid the consequence. I was disciplined enough to get up early and read the Bible and pray. I was disciplined enough to get up early and exercise. I was not disciplined with my thoughts. (2 Corinthians 10:5) I was allowing the thoughts that the enemy was putting in my mind to be my truth. I was allowing him to dictate my connection and intimacy with my husband. And for years, I didn't think I could control it. I honestly did not. I thought, "This is the way I am wired. These are things I can't get over and we will just have to live like this, incomplete and lacking what God probably wants for us."

A few years ago, I found myself overwhelmed and defeated. The Lord showed me an amazing opportunity to be an online lifestyle coach to help other women and men learn to live a realistic, sustainable, and healthy lifestyle. I had personally created some healthy habits of my own while working long hours with small kids, and now I had the chance to pay it forward to others. This was actually one of the most exciting things I have ever said yes to because it has been a dream job that I still enjoy to this day. I run my own business, work when I am able, am present for my kids, leave the daily grind of working for someone else, share Jesus in a unique way, and have a long-term, healthy, FIT family to share life with. ABSOLUTELY PERFECT. Except for someone like me who already subconsciously identified myself as a failure, working for yourself requires lots of obstacles, objections, trial and error, and long hours as well.

Women and men who were struggling and insecure with themselves, who had lost hope or didn't trust themselves, looked to me for help and trusted that I would help them. I was depending on helping them and earning income this way was hard. Like really hard. Soon after I said YES to making this a full-time gig, things got hard. Goals that I had set out for myself seemed impossible or didn't happen, and I received lots and lots of no's. I soon began to focus on all the things that were not going right and how much I was failing. Almost instantly my intellectual insecurities I had faced my entire life started to become something the enemy was using to explain why my business wasn't working and why people didn't trust me. I began to revert back to an insecure, negative mindset. This directly impacted my mind and the actions I would take every day.

I had moments that I quit believing in myself and I doubted my purpose and God's plan. All the insecurities from when I had failed my medical certification exams while in college and other instances that I had failed swarmed my mind. I would spend hours and even days questioning everything about my life and my capabilities. I was believing the lies that the enemy was feeding me.

But then I am reminded of God's faithfulness.

Yes, some of the things I have endured emotionally have been devastating and pierced my heart. Yes, I still deal with some of the scars as the enemy tries to open wounds. But God was faithful. God showed up every day for me and brought me through. I look back and think, "What are the odds of someone with learning disabilities completing medical school, and writing books?" But where there is a will, there is always a way with God. Every time I doubt, I have to remind myself of who HE is, not what I am not. Worrying about how things will turn out and how I will be able to do things only leaves room for the enemy to work.

God gives us the exact energy we need to face the day and fulfill his plan: don't waste any on worrying. If you spend all your time worrying, you'll never get prepared. God has provided a way where our past has ZERO power over us, but we must receive HIS unconditional love and gift of forgiveness and mercy

What if all you have been through is not so that you feel rejected, abused, forgotten, unloved, and unvalued? What if all you have been through was a gift? Whoever said that a gift was without pain or sacrifice? Jesus died on the cross; he was punctured, wounded, and pierced in pain to give us the gift of life. He endured it all, FOR YOU! So, what if the circumstance, the things of your past, were actually a gift? Something that you can actually use to become WHO you were created to be?

Chapter 13

No More Hot Mess: It's Time to Rise Up and Fight

Below are some affirming statements and Scripture references that help remind me WHOSE I AM. It's like a personal pep talk, an intimate conversation with myself and God. Exchange my name for your name and read out these statements. Better yet, write them in your own journal for added reinforcement.

Stay alert! Life is never guaranteed to be easy, especially when you are walking in obedience to the Lord. Watch out for the great enemy, the devil. He prowls around like a roaring lion, looking for someone to devour (1 Peter 5:8)

You need to be prepared. Trust and know that God is strong and he makes you strong! When you start to think negative thoughts and doubt, take everything He has been telling you, the things you are learning in his word, and hold onto everything. Be prepared to use them like well-made weapons. His Word (2 Timothy3:16-17), your direct, divine lifeline, prayer (James 1:5), your shield of faith, they are there for you to use! Put them to use so you will be able to stand up to everything the devil throws your way! (Ephesians 6:10-17)

When you become overwhelmed and forget who is in control and forget whose you are, STOP! Be grateful! Before you are overwhelmed with life and its circumstances, be sure that whatever you do or say is a representation of the Lord! (Colossians 3:17)

And when things are not going the way you planned, when you start to question why and how, you leave little energy and room for the Lord in today and today is what matters. (Matthew 6:34)

Focus on today and all that is good. And if you can't find anything good, remember how loved you are. Thank God for showing you how much he loves you and for sending His son to die for you even though we didn't deserve it (Romans 5:8)

There will be days when you are frustrated with yourself, with your quirks, your shortcomings, even the way you are wired, but remember that you were made on purpose. Remember God has a plan and you are part of it. Thank you, God, for making me so wonderfully complex! Your workmanship is marvelous – how well I know it. (Psalm 139:14) Thank you for making me into your masterpiece God, creating me anew in Christ Jesus, and specifically to do the good things you planned for me long ago. (Ephesians 2:10)

Some days it will seem like you have everything under control, which is a tendency to want this every day. But then we leave no room for Jesus. So on the days that seem out of control, be careful how you think, because your life is shaped by your thoughts. (Proverbs 4:23)

And even on the days that negativity and doubt envelop my mind, Lord remind me of your goodness. Thank you, God, for being so patient and kind! When I don't feel capable, you remind me that you called me to share in your glory! I know that ultimately, NO MATTER what I feel about myself, no matter what I am going through or am experiencing, you will restore my soul! You will support me and strengthen me and realign me on a firm foundation! (1 Peter 5:10)
Above all, lean into Jesus so that you can learn to live out your faith and trust in God. The more time you spend with Him, the more you understand His ways. (Matthew 6:33) For

the Lord is the Spirit, and wherever the Spirit of the Lord is, there is freedom (2 Corinthians 3:17)

Listen, the Lord wants to do something new. Hello... don't you see it?! He will make a pathway through the wilderness. He will create rivers in the dry wasteland! (Isaiah 43:19) Do not lose hope.

Trust me! I am your unshakable, unmovable, and eternal ROCK (Isaiah 26:4)
I am here to protect you, shield you, and be your safe place!

I know at times you feel alone, even lost, but I've already showed up for you as I promised and will bring you back to me, your home! I have never left. I know what I'm doing. I have it all planned out: I am taking care of you, I have not abandoned you! (Deuteronomy 31:6)

Trust me! I have a plan to give you the future that you have hoped for. (Jeremiah 29:10-11)

Maybe instead of being so focused on my selfish position, my comfort, I should ask: How do you want me to be, God? How do you want me to be in this situation? Help me to learn to fully trust, and instead of asking what do you want me to do God help me to focus on my disposition towards you and the situation (2 Timothy 3: 16-17).

After reading and writing these prayers, this conversation with God, where do you find yourself?

Maybe you are wanting the blessing, but you are not willing to do the work. Maybe you have been seeking, but you have already made up your mind that you can't or you don't want to. Acts 28:27 says, "For the hearts of the people have grown dull. Their ears are hard of hearing, and their eyes closed, lest they should see their eyes and hear with their ears, lest they should understand with their hearts and turn so that I should heal them."

We have to be willing to hear the answer we are being given. WE HAVE TO BE WILLING TO HEAR THE ANSWER! And sometimes this answer is not what we want to hear, but it is the exact thing we need and should do.

Asking God to speak and asking God to show up doesn't mean that we get to choose the way He shows up or choose what He tells us to do. So often we are begging and praying, but we have already put restrictions and limitations on our God, putting a shield up to even receive what he's trying to tell us.

We want easy, we want the least resistance, we want what we want, and so often if we don't like the answer we are given, we pretend it's not from God. This makes us feel better about why we aren't taking action. But of course, this causes us to fall back into our selfish ways, the "I want" and "I need" and eventually we start feeling alone, isolated, and even believing that God has forgotten us because we are not getting what we "have prayed for" or what we think we want or need. We've conditioned ourselves to believe that life needs to be easy or streamline or it isn't from God.

If God has told you to step up your love, attention, and efforts in marriage, but you DO NOT WANT to, sister, you need to do what He asked. I know, trust me, I've said myself, "He needs to give me attention, he needs to do this, it's him that isn't loving and giving me the attention I NEED." Yes, this may be true, but YOU are the one with the issues about

181

it. So lean into this longing and request of your father. And YES, this is your answer to prayer: YOU taking action. For example, if you have found yourself miserable, uncomfortable, and knowing that you need to get healthier, you and I both know this will require some sort of action. To feel better, to gain confidence, and to have what you need to live out all that God has called you to do, you will need to take action. This is exactly what God has called you to, to do what's necessary to get healthy.

NO sister, he didn't call you to take the easiest, quickest path of least resistance in hopes that you will lose 10lbs in one week and BE ALL THAT GOD CREATED YOU TO BE. No, this doesn't happen like this. Never will! All of the circumstances and calls to action by your heavenly father will take getting uncomfortable in your faith, they will take work.

There is one thing that I heard once and will never forget, and honestly, it's shaped a lot of my beliefs. If I am presented with an option, a vision, a task, or something that I know I need to do, the most difficult, the hardest, the one that seems impossible, THAT'S the thing that God is calling us to! WHY? Because it will require HIM to be completely involved. It will require more of Him than me. And that, my dear sister, is exactly WHAT our life is supposed to be about. If you have been praying about something, most likely you have already been given an answer, you just don't like it and are hoping for an easier way.

And like I said, easy is usually not of the Lord, because otherwise you wouldn't need Him. Have you been leaning on your own understanding to figure things out?

I will never forget one of the first times that my husband and I went rock climbing. It was not in the Colorado Rockies, but a swanky indoor place full of what seemed to be experts. Now I am the adventurous one. I love a challenge and doing new things. But for some reason, as I get older, I have found my heart racing a bit more when I approach things of great height. Perhaps it's because I am giving myself as many opportunities to take risks with my life.

This rock climbing adventure not only took me beyond my comfort level for height, but it also left me in the hands of my husband, who would be operating the lever as I was lowered to the ground. Trusting my husband to not let go, that I wouldn't fall, that it would all go as planned, I am not going to lie, that made my heart rate go up. But y'all, I was at the top and there was only one way down. A few ways to get there, but ultimately, I was coming down. I had to fully trust that my husband would get me down safely. I was in a situation where I knew my husband was capable of operating the equipment, I knew he was strong enough to do the job, but even beyond that, I had to jump. He was there, at the bottom, waiting, but I had to let him lower me down. I had to trust and then let him do what he was trained to do.

You see, God's strength is available to us too, just like with my husband. But even though it is available, it was only tangible for me since I was willing to let him help me down. God is the same way. He is here all the time, ready and available to help us, but only to those who are willing to use his help! We have to be fully willing to jump, to take action, otherwise we never jump into how the Lord can work. Refusing to jump and refusing to trust doesn't change God, it just means we miss out on His miraculous plan and the work he wants to do in and through us.

Proverbs 3 reminds us to trust in the Lord from the bottom of your heart; don't try and figure it out on your own, listen to God's voice in everything you do, everywhere you go, he's the one who will keep you on track. Don't assume that you know it all. Don't resent God's discipline or run from the hard stuff. Don't sulk when you are being redirected or when you feel your refining is too much. For the child he loved much, he corrects much. (Hebrews 12:6)

Are you tired of hanging on to whatever it is that is pulling you away from God?

Are you willing to jump, to cling onto him and trust that God has you?

Chapter 14
Believe in Miracles

In order to change your life and start living a new one, your faith in miracles and yourself and your God must be bigger than your fears.

Surrender is the part where you hand the job over to God. And it's not about throwing your hands up before someone who is out to get you, but rather giving your life to the one who loves you. How is your posture?

Is it:
Trusting
Faithful
Obedient
Patient
Believing
Gracious
Loving

If you are broke as a joke, overweight, overwhelmed, struggling to survive the day, or have decided to settle because you've decided you don't have the energy or willpower to give any more, then here's the gift we've all been desperately waiting for! We don't have to fix the problem. I didn't say we don't have to do anything, I said we don't have to fix it! Our job isn't to figure out the how, it's to embrace the NOW! It's about recognizing what's available to us now and what we can do with what we have now.

It's about showing up NOW, with an excellent attitude, doing the best we can, choosing to celebrate any and all victories and being grateful and living in expectation that God is here, guiding us, and providing us with every single need. He has our back! It's about a choice to trust and believe! Trust that figuring everything out and fixing everything is NOT our responsibility, but showing up because we believe in His power and plan IS!

Swap the why not, the how for the NOW! No more pity parties, keep your desires strong and faith unwavering! Doubt means you resist, you automatically decided in disobedience. Faith positions us for goodness. When we surrender, we allow ourselves to experience things out of our control and these things are called miracles.

Believe. Truly position your heart, mind, thoughts, and your entire being to a place of belief! I pray that at this point that you have decided that you truly believe. Fall into His love, His care, His promises with unwavering faith with gratitude and begin to unapologetically live out this faith.

John 8:32
Hold onto me and what I say about you. For my words are your truth and the essence of what you were created to be! And it is then, sister, when you know these truths and live them, that you are then set free! His truth, your truth, will set you free!

I also appreciate the message in James 1:1-12.

And lastly, in 1 John 4:4, "My dear children, you come from God and belong to God. You have already won a big victory over those false teachers, for the Spirit in you is far stronger than anything in the world."

#NOMOREHOTMESS

You are Brave

You are Strong

You are an Overcomer

You are a Conquer

You are loved

You are disciplined

You are worthy

You are a wonderful mother

You are a great wife

You have a great marriage.

You are worth more than a paycheck

You are worth more than the opinions of others

You don't need permission to live your truth and live in freedom.

How to quit the Hot Mess

Charge #1

In Hebrews 6:1-3, God used the writer of Hebrews to give us a charge, to give us instruction on how to quit the hotmess life and live the freedom life.

We are to hold fast to the truth of who we are and to go on in maturity.

Through time with Him daily, through doing the hard stuff, through learning and growing, through pain and frustration, through our past, we are being made mature, complete in him.

He said to leave the preschool fingerpainting behind and get on with the grand work of art. Leave the excuses, your old thoughts, your old way of living, and grow up in Christ.

Like we talked about before, we know that we can't grow up in Christ if we don't do what he is asking us to do.

He says recognize it and turn away from self-help salvation. Stop trying to self-medicate, stop trying to fix it all and figure it all out. Stop with the quick solutions and feel good cupcakes.

Instead, sister, we must turn towards God.

When we realize that we are fulling living up to the hotmess life, stop and look up.

He is the way. He is the only thing that will satisfy. He is the only one with all the right answers. He is the same yesterday, today, and forever (Hebrews 13:8)

There should be a consistency that runs through all of us. Just as Jesus doesn't change: yesterday, today, tomorrow, he's always totally himself, so should we stay consistent. Don't be lured away from him by the latest speculations about him. The grace of Christ is the only good ground for life.

He is the peace you need.

He is the love that you are longing for.

He is the validation you need.

He is FREEDOM.

When you KNOW Jesus, his love for you, his promises for your future, you CAN and want to act differently. (Romans 6:15-17) The way you live comes from a different place; A place beyond self.

If you are changed and you BELIEVE in him and trust him, you walk in bold faith.

If you haven't realized it, your hotmess is always going to try and cover up your truth, deceive you and try to do everything he can to keep you from peace and freedom. Every day this battle will rage. The spiritual war will rage. The true issue is not the food, your lack of discipline, your husband, your kids, your illness, or your past. *The issue is the enemy doing EVERYTHING he can to keep you a mess.*

We will be tempted to let the old weeds, cluttered house, missing socks, donut you ate, old feelings of rejection you feel from your husband, and never-ending to-do list be the dictator of our lives. We will continue to be pulled to let our mess win. We might even unapologetically wear the t-shirt because that's how we feel some days.

But the truth is, because of the spirit in us, God in us, we are more POWERFUL than our mess. We are so much more than our mess.

God says I have better things in mind for you: salvation things! Redemption things. Freedom things.

God sees it all, knows it all, and he doesn't miss anything. He knows perfectly well all the love you have shown him by showing up, by hustling and helping others, and he sees you keep at it. He sees your tired and weary soul.

But because you know his love, the truth of how much he loves you, and you BELIEVE what he has promised you, you can extend the same intensity towards full-bodied hope and keep at it till the finish. (1 Corinthians 9:24-27) Put your energy into this HOPE. Celebrate it, focus on it and let this hope shine brighter than your mess.

You have Him to help you! You have His strength, His boldness, His discipline. All that is lacking, lacks no more.

So sister, Don't drag your feet. Don't wait, don't delay. No more doubting.

Be like those who stay the course and then get everything promised to them.

He promised peace and freedom when you do things His way.

Boldly walk in HIS truth every day.

I affirm my truth daily and I BELIEVE that is who I am. It is who I am.

Charge #2

There should be a consistency that runs through all of us, just as Jesus doesn't change- yesterday, today, tomorrow. (Hebrews 13:8)

Because we know His truth and the way to freedom, be empowered to get up and go, to do what you know you are being called to do, and sister, believe you can be all that you were created to be. Consistently. You don't have to do this half-way, and certainly not only when you feel like it or only when someone returns the favor. DO not have expectations.

But show up because you believe that it matters.

You know He has gone before you.

What if he created you for SUCH A TIME AS THIS.

What if this exact thing or things that you are struggling with will bring you closer to the peace you have been longing for.

What if your growth produces fruit that allows you to shine light that points someone to Jesus.

Because at the end of the day, our walk, our journey, YOUR STORY, is God's story. He invited us to partner with Him in His work here on earth, to be the light pointing others to Him.

So your life, your obedience, is really not about YOU sister!

Lord knows a hotmess can't even see straight. So this is why we can't live there. This is why we must understand that this is not who we are.

In 2 Corinthians 5:17, Paul says, "Therefore if anyone is in Christ, he is a new creation; the old has gone and new has come."

New doesn't mean we upgrade from a hotmess to a partialmess, or that God temporarily forgave and forgot until we mess up again.

Sister. When you said yes to Jesus, you said yes to a NEW CREATION.

Brand-spankin' new. God put a new self inside of you. He literally took your hotmess self and placed His Holy Spirit there.

This means that our nature is NOW His nature.

Don't overlook the obvious and slip back into the hotmess by thinking that you really aren't that different and all you really need to do is behave differently, "more Christian-like."

Remember, your messy self wants you to be in constant war with yourself. Trying to measure up, trying to do more to feel better, trying to please, trying to fix. Grasping for something or someone to fix you or your mess.

Or if you keep circling the same mountain, you end up hoping the hotmess will eventually go away and the new you will take over and you won't have to deal with it anymore.

The enemy wants to keep the hotmess alive and unsettled, longing, striving, and with the all-so-familiar anxiousness. He wants you here because this is where you will stay.

He wants us to keep fighting a battle that has already been won.

But the NEW YOU, the REAL YOU can now stand up in bold faith and confidence! In BELIEF.

God is not afraid of our mess! He calls us to step out of the shadows of the mess. To quit hiding and run to him.

So yes, sister, you can be messy and live among the mess of a life.

But you, my dear friend, are not a hotmess. The inner voice telling you that you shouldn't live like one, it's real. That's Jesus calling.

And if you would just look up, you would know he wants to tell you that you are that decedent, red velvet cupcake with buttercream frosting and sprinkles and you are filled with the good, creamy stuff, too.

You are the good stuff. You are EVERYTHING God says you are.

No matter what's going on around you, what's going on within you, what your hotmess is trying to get you to believe, you ARE already complete!

I love you dearly!

I am thankful to be on this journey with you! I am honored to get to encourage and motivate you through His love and grace.

Cheneil

Chapter 14

I am NOT a HotMess!

I am smart

I am worthy

I am a world changer

I am brave and courageous

I am fearfully and wonderfully made

I am called by God to do great things

I am clothed in God's strength

I stand strong in the face of adversity.

I can't stop running because Jesus didn't stop running after me.

I am a finisher.

I am the right woman for this job.

I am a winner.

I am unconditionally loved.

I am a great mom.

I am rooted and grounded in love and truth.

I am richly blessed, and I am blessing others.

I am abundantly graced.

I am my brother and sister's keeper.

I am a loving wife.

I am empowered to take the lead.

I am an overcomer.

Greater is he that is in me than he that is in the world.

I am a daughter of the King

No matter how I feel and no matter how it looks, I will see His promises manifested in my life.

I am patient and kind

I am truthful.

I am hidden in Christ.

I was born for such a time as this.

I have what it takes.

I am resourceful

I am wise.

I laugh without fear of the future.

I am highly favored.

I am victorious.

I wear God's grace and beauty.

I live on the promises of what God said he would do through me, not on the basis of what I can do.

I am crowned!

I am Royalty!

I am not a HotMess, I am FREE!

Chapter 14

No More Hot Mess

No More Hot Mess

About the Author

Cheneil is a full-time professional motivator, faith-based lifestyle coach, mentor, and speaker. She resides in Texas with her husband of 14 years and two young boys. She is an outgoing, energetic, daughter of the King who loves fitness and Jesus. She is passionate about helping women like you understand God's truth, His unconditional, unwavering love for you, and helping you see it and live in it out in the midst of your everyday messy life. Through her time caring for patients as a Certified Acute Care Nurse Practitioner for over a decade, the Lord started to reveal His truth to her in a defining, real, and raw way, and in the midst of a messy, exhausting, and dry time in her life God shared with her His new plan and purpose for her.

Cheneil's heart is for YOU, encouraging you, and motivating you through your mess. Because it's through this mess that God is making Miracles. She shares her heart and passion with you in many ways:

- Monthly Interactive Faith Calendar: includes a community of women who need a plan, encouragement, and accountability.
- Individualized Faith-Based Online Lifestyle Coaching to help you on a more personal level.
- Motivational Faith-Based Speaking on Lifestyle & Healthy Living for your next Women's event.
- You can find more about her services at cheneiltorbert.com or follow her on Facebook or IG.

Motivating you through His Grace & Love
Cheneil

No More Hot Mess

No More Hot Mess

No More Hot Mess

Disclaimer & Copyright Information

Some of the events, details, and conversations have been recreated from memories. In order to maintain their anonymity, in some instances, the names of individuals and places have been changed. As such, some identifying characteristics and details may have changed.

Although the author and publisher have made every effort to ensure that the information in this book was correct at press time, the author and publisher do not assume and hereby disclaim any liability to any party for any loss, damage, or disruption caused by errors or omissions, whether such errors or omissions result from negligence, accident, or any other cause. The author is solely responsible for the content contained in this book.

All quotes, unless otherwise noted,
are attributed to the respective author or to the Holy Bible.

NOTES

NOTES